The Clashing Worlds of Economics and Faith

James Halteman

Wipf & Stock
PUBLISHERS
Eugene, Oregon

Wipf and Stock Publishers
199 W 8th Ave, Suite 3
Eugene, OR 97401

The Clashing Worlds of Economics and Faith
By Halteman, James
Copyright©1995 Herald Press
ISBN 13: 978-1-55635-170-9
ISBN 10: 1-55635-170-4
Publication date: 1/3/2007
Previously published by Herald Press, 1995

Reproduced by permission of Herald Press

This is a renamed, revised, and expanded edition of *Market Capitalism and Christianity,* Grand Rapids: Baker Book House, 1988.

To my mother and father,
Wilmer and Perle Halteman,
who never preached stewardship;
they just practiced it.

Contents

Foreword

I have taught Principles of Economics at a Christian college for more than forty years. Because my course was a general education elective for many students as well as a requirement for majors, I wanted to be sure that I taught it from a Christian standpoint. However, I was often at a loss to know how I could in fact teach not only economics but Christian economics. A line between mathematics and Christian mathematics is often difficult to draw because of the abstract nature of mathematics. However, all economics has a social component. It is important that the teacher of economics recognizes this. Consequently, I longed for a book of supplementary readings which would provide this element. Now one of my students offers herewith precisely the kind of book I had wished for.

Yet James Halteman's new volume should enjoy a far wider readership than beginning students of economics in a Christian college. Anyone engaged in business will find in this new book ways in which one's business can be operated more in accord with Christian principles. The same principles apply also to those in the professions. Indeed, I think they are significant for all of us.

The Bible has much to teach about economics. The Old Testament prophets made rigorous demands on their hearers. But the demands are even more explicit in the teachings of Jesus. In fact, Jesus had more to say about question of economics than about most other moral issues. How shall we interpret Jesus' requirement for one of his would-be followers: "Sell all that you own and distribute the money to the poor" (Luke 18:22)? Few of us would be willing to follow this literally. Many find it difficult to give even the tithe.

5

Halteman rightly asks that Christians not only pray for the revelation of God's will as they personally struggle for answers to these questions. They should also seek the counsel of other Christians in the church. Through group discernment, Halteman believes, the Christian will find answers to questions such as how much we should give. Furthermore, group counsel will illuminate all of Jesus' teachings on economic matters. A congregation of four hundred will probably be too large a reference group for discerning Jesus' will on implementing his radical demands. But within a congregation of any size, small groups of ten to twelve will be most effective. He supports this with his own personal experience and with the examples of others as well.

A major difference between the economy of our day and that of Jesus' day is that productive capital is now of crucial importance for the economy as a whole. A Christian businessperson today saves not to satisfy greedy future wants—as implied in Jesus' parable of the rich man tearing down his barns to build larger ones so that he ultimately could eat, drink, and be merry. Saving today stems from a desire to enhance the welfare of the whole community by enlarging the stock of productive capital.

Halteman's book examines many other issues confronted in the clash between economics and Christian faith. His analysis makes a highly important contribution to the continuing discussion. I recommend this book with enthusiasm.

Carl Kreider
Dean Emeritus
Goshen College

Preface

Much has changed since the earlier version of this book was written nearly eight years ago. As I passed the tanks poised before the "White House" in Moscow on August 15, 1991, I did not comprehend the significance of the coup that I was watching. A few days later when I exited the subway station near the "White House" to join in celebrating the downfall of what those tanks had stood for, I only began to sense that much of what I believed about economics and social organization was about to be tested.

But the earlier years of the 1990s involved far more than the downfall of authoritarian central planning in the Soviet Union and Eastern Europe. Something even more foundational was happening in how we think. Modern economics, like many other areas of study, was developed in a world that thought there were answers to all problems. The 18th century was a time to explore the orderly creation and find out its patterns so that we could reach some optimal harmonious grand theory of how the world worked. This exploration we called science, and it was supposed to hold the keys to the truth of the universe. Economics jumped on this band wagon, thinking that, with correct theory, we could create a new economic world order. That order was called free market capitalism.

The irony of this story so far is that the downfall of communism has not led to the triumphal onward march of capitalism. In fact, the capitalist successes of this century are becoming mired in an array of problems that are leading to fragmentation in theory and practice. The search for a grand theory that would explain how the world functions is a task that thinkers are beginning to give up. In physics and philosophy, in literature and theology, the voices are starting to sound the same. Uncertainty, contradiction, paradox, disequilibrium, and chaos are replacing their opposites. Themes like coping rather than conquering are becoming standard fare in professional and popular literature.

The neat models showing the way the world works and pre-scribing how we can benefit from the order of the universe are now becoming suspect. The modern world, as we called it, is giving way to the "postmodern" world which offers little hope that we can grasp objective truth in any area of life. What is left is a sense of disillusionment and confusion that neither economics nor Christianity can escape. It's not that free markets are failing to be an engine for economic growth and development. Rather, the problem is that growth and development, while providing comfort, are not bringing meaning and peace to people.

Consequently, this version of the book will take a closer look to see how capitalism can be integrated with an active Christian faith. Most of the revisions come in the sections dealing with market theory and practice. The sections on Christian practice are changed little. The most common critique of the earlier work was that it was too idealistic in its recommendations about how believers should live in economic life. It is my view that the more society fragments into a postmodern way of thinking, the more Christians will feel like strangers and pilgrims in a foreign land. We will be forced to be more serious and intentional about how we live out our faith.

Despite the effort of many Christians to reform the world for Christ, the postmodern world is also post-Christian. Therefore, reform efforts will become increasingly ineffective. In this environment, believers will have no place to turn but to their communities of faith. The option of Christian countercultural living will then be more easily seen as a viable witness to the world. Indeed, in a truly postmodern post-Christian world, the suggestions presented in this book may seem tame if not inadequate.

There is no way to adequately thank all those who contributed to this expanded and updated version of the earlier book. My visits with college classes and church groups of all kinds have helped me see how the content of that book came across to non-economists. Pastors have helped me see how laymen responded to some of the more controversial ideas that made their way into sermons. Also, it was my good fortune to have a scholar-editor shepherd the manuscript through the various drafts. S. David Garber performed this function for Herald Press and the book is stronger because of his biblical expertise. In short, this book is appropriately a community project which hopefully can stimulate further dialogue for the glory of God.

It is humbling to write about things that are not easy to practice. I am in process as a believer, and so I find the Christian walk to be both rewarding and frustrating at the same time. I still find 1 Corinthians 13 to be a favorite text, not because of the beautiful poetic content that shows the dynamics of a successful community of faith, but rather because of verse 12. "For now we see in a mirror, dimly, but then we will see face to face. Now I know only in part; then I will know fully, even as I have been fully known." Perhaps this effort to focus the poor reflection a bit more sharply can be helpful as we seek to be more faithful Christians.

James Halteman
Wheaton College

Introduction

M y standard of living is no one's business but my own."
"It is not wealth, but the love of wealth that matters."
"The Bible teaches against accumulated wealth."

"Market capitalism is the only economic system a Christian
should support."

"Scriptural teaching on economic matters is directed toward
an agricultural no-growth environment and therefore is not very
relevant today."

"The Christian's primary task is to infiltrate the economic
structures of the world to win them for Christ."

Over the years these statements, or variations of them, have
surfaced again and again in many settings. Simple responses to
them have never seemed adequate. Discussions of these statements invariably lead to theological and economic issues that
create endless debate. Thus my attempt to deal with these and
other issues relating to the Christian faith and economics is not
without some risk. I hope that throughout the book the challenges
to faithful stewardship will come through in a helpful way.

My training as an economist and my study of biblical and
theological material represent only part of the background material for this book. Perhaps the most compelling source has been
my experience in the community of faith at various places. Over
the last several decades, I have come to believe that the desire for
self-sufficiency and autonomy is a stumbling block for believers.
My most inspiring challenge has been to help build the church at
the levels of congregation, conference, and denomination. I am
more convinced now than ever that the economics of the Bible can

10

best be understood in the context of a community of faith. Both the Old Testament and the New seem to proclaim that message from beginning to end. At the same time I am not optimistic that any secular economic system can provide true economic well-being. Market capitalism can deliver goods and services in amazing quantities, but it cannot guarantee caring communities that sustain body and spirit. In fact, despair and loneliness lurk amid the plenty, and competitive capitalism has not been able to erase them. The Christian faith offers an answer to this despair, but it is not a simple, easy cure. Christian people need a strategy that will help them to be true to Scripture and to be responsible stewards of resources. This book suggests such a strategy.

There are two agendas for the Christian to pursue. First, the believer should help the church design and practice the kind of economic behavior that will witness to the emerging kingdom of God. This witness is not a utopian dream, but an exciting possibility for all believers. It can also be a powerful–though largely untapped–tool of evangelism.

Second, the believer needs to understand and influence the secular capitalistic system of which Western Christians are a part. This involves the difficult task of connecting two ideologies that have limited compatibility. In other words, the community of faith must practice biblical values together while it interacts in a secular world that has different goals.

The tension believers experience between the two agendas is depicted by this continuum:

├───┤

Modelers: Practicing val-   *Infiltrators*: Influencing
ues of the kingdom of God   values of the secular
                                 system

Modelers, as they are called here, believe that Christians have a . special calling to practice values not common in a secular world. They believe that being in the world but not of the world has specific implications for life. Infiltrators, in contrast, see the Christian task primarily as infiltrating the structures of society to influence people and social institutions for good.

Infiltrators criticize modelers, believing they are too uninvolved in social structures. They believe that modelers' efforts to live out the teachings of the kingdom of God in the real world are utopian and lead to an ineffective outward ministry. In contrast, modelers see infiltrators as compromisers who sell out to the world. They argue that infiltrators have lost the radical calling of the gospel and have adopted the world's standards of success and power.

Obviously, I have described the extremes of the continuum. In reality, most believers live between the extremes. However, it is a thesis of this book that believers today have moved too far to the infiltrator side of the continuum and need to feel a tug back toward the modeling side. There will always be tension pulling a believer from both sides of the continuum as long as we "see in a mirror, dimly," but there are times when circumstances make us more susceptible to err on one side or the other. The pluralistic, tolerant society in which we live, the material well-being that many believers enjoy, and the moral relativism of our time have made infiltration the easy alternative in the latter half of the twentieth century in much of the capitalistic Western world.

This book has four related parts. First, it discusses the essentials of any economic system. All economic systems must perform the tasks of allocation and production. To do so, they must be organized in some fashion consistent with the values and social patterns of their society. The worldview of the times provides a framework for the kinds of institutional structures that seem plausible in a particular time and place. We must understand this background before we can be prepared to consider any specific methods of economic organization.

Second, the book sketches the kind of economic relationships a modeler might propose for the community of believers and presents some simple hermeneutical and theological considerations to set the stage for the model.

Third, the book considers the economic world that Western Christians are attempting to infiltrate. It explores three pillars of market capitalism in order to understand the differences between values of the kingdom of God and values of the secular institutions of Western market economies.

Fourth, the book suggests ways for the community of faith to interact effectively with market capitalism without selling out to its spirit. To model without becoming isolated and to infiltrate without selling out to the world are the ideals to which this book points, whether the world we face is modern or postmodern.

Two groups of people will benefit most from this book. The first consists of students beginning the study of economics. The part on market capitalism will help to give an intuitive sense of what economics is all about and how capitalism solves economic problems. The part that sketches the economics of the believers church will challenge the student to evaluate economic behavior in light of biblical content. The conclusions are controversial and should foster constructive debate. The discussion questions at the end of each chapter help to focus the issues involved in each topic.

The second audience consists of people interested in policy issues from a biblical perspective who have little economic training. The perspective on market capitalism presented here should be useful for ministers and laypeople alike who seek viewpoints on various economic concerns.

This book represents an Anabaptist approach to Christian practice. The two-kingdom model developed in chapter 4 contrasts with the alternate view that any Christian model must be generally applicable to believers and nonbelievers alike because all of creation must be subject to the moral will of the same Creator. Anabaptist thought has always had countercultural threads that challenge believers to a life of discipleship that does not make sense to unbelievers. This counterculture discipleship works best in the context of a community of faith that supports believers seeking to be faithful. Readers from both Anabaptist and non-Anabaptist traditions should find this book helpful for dialogue in the search for consistent ways to follow Scripture in economic life.

1

The Economic Context

E conomics exists because we live in a world where people can not have all they want of everything free. This situation is present no matter where we live, what century we live in, or how plentiful our resources are. To illustrate how pervasive this problem is, imagine a world where there is an abundance of everything and all resources are free. What will you do? No doubt you will act like the shopper who can have anything at zero price so long as one selects and brings it to the checkout counter in fifteen minutes. The shopper immediately experiences a strong sense of scarcity even though all the products are free. Why? Because suddenly time is scarce and must be allocated carefully. If the shopper ends up with the perfect market basket, it is because–perhaps unconsciously–sound economic reasoning was used in allocating the time. Only in a timeless heaven is economics obsolete.

If we give the shopper two constraints, the problem more closely approximates the real world. Suppose the shopper has fifteen minutes, one hundred dollars, and cannot ignore prices. Now the venture becomes more difficult; more decisions are necessary. Time is scarce and resources are scarce–a fact communicated by the assigned prices. Scarcity in this example illustrates the dilemma that we all find ourselves in every day. We have limited time and resources, while our imaginations can dream up endless wants to fulfill. This condition is as true for twentieth-century Americans as it was for the ancient world of the Hebrews and the first-century world of Jesus. The economic problem is universal.

To say we live in a world where things are not free (economists call this a world of scarcity) is not to say that the world is incapable of providing enough to keep humanity alive and well. Rather, it means that people cannot have all they desire at a price they can afford. In a world where people's wants are minimal and their productivity high, scarcity could be eliminated. However, that world has not yet been found. I suggest later in this book that Christian people should develop the concept of limited wants. But the controversy that this suggestion usually creates among believers is proof enough that a secular concept of limited wants is far from a reality.

Economic decisions, then, are made within the framework of scarcity. Any system must allocate limited resources among an endless list of desires in ways that are consistent with the values of the society, foster adequate production, and accommodate needed change. All systems, whether small or large, must deal with these issues if they hope to survive.

It is helpful at this point to depict the requirements of an economic system (see figure 1.1).

Figure 1.1
The Context of Economic Systems

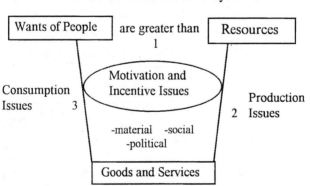

The upper two boxes illustrate that people live in a world of scarcity. They have endless wants and limited resources and time, so they must find a way to cope with the problem. Three major ways present themselves. First, a partial solution would be to scale down the wants to make the gap between wants and resources feel smaller. If society moved toward a simple-lifestyle norm that made minimal resource use socially desirable, the gap between wants and available resources would become smaller. Since per capita economic growth was not an expected outcome of economic behavior throughout most of history, it is easy to understand why Jesus, in the first century, was oriented more toward conservation and redistribution than toward expanded production. Improving production process could be a second approach to solving the economic question. Third, the method of allocating available goods and services among consumers can be improved so that products go to their best uses. It is important to understand all three components of this economic context triangle because each side has its own set of issues. Each side is numbered for clarity.

Side 1 represents all the concerns associated with scaling down *living standards* and coping with a steady-state economic environment. In most societies this conservation approach is not popular because it is thought to cause unemployment or at least to slow economic growth. In the secular world of Western market capitalism, where desires are an individual matter and personal autonomy is a primary goal, most people prefer more to less. Countering this natural tendency is considered an unacceptable act of coercion. This option will be considered later when we look at Christian alternatives.

Side 2 of the triangle deals with issues of *production* economics. Discovering more resources and processing them more effectively are the tasks of those who tackle the scarcity problem from this angle. The technological change and constantly expanding productivity of the modern world help make this option seem plausible.

Side 3 is concerned with finding the best way to get goods and services to their best uses in *consumption*. It has to do with how goods and services are distributed among the millions of people who want them. Why should this home go to this family and not to that? Why should that pair of slacks go to that consumer and not to another? How best can we determine who ought to enjoy a given service of which there isn't enough for everyone?

If the allocation side of the triangle is putting products to their best use and if the production side is using the best resource mix to produce the right goods, then the economy is doing its job. In fact, economics as a discipline is really the study of ways to tie together the entire triangle into a system that allocates scarce resources and products to make them serve people. In much of the Western world, that system is democratic capitalism, a system often unfairly maligned, sometimes oversold, and usually only vaguely understood. Finding a system that meets the needs of society and fits the values of the Christian faith is a difficult challenge. The two-kingdom approach of this book suggests that this challenge may be too great to solve.

In the ancient Hebrew world of the Old Testament, the economic triangle was dealt with in the context of the law and the community of faith. A theocracy with revealed law, a prescribed social organization, and a covenant relationship with Yahweh answered the economic questions in some detail.

In the earlier period of Roman rule, the triangle was organized by the law of a central authority, from which subjects deviated at their own risk. In Jesus' day, economic behavior was regulated by power beyond the control of the Jewish people, who were forced to sacrifice to Rome most of any significant surplus they could generate. Thus the believer's economic behavior occurred in a framework of limited options. The persecuted believer had virtually no voice in the creation of social institutions and practice. The teachings of Jesus and the New Testament writers are best understood against this backdrop, and it is easy to see why Jesus said little about the explicit design of the social order.

Although he challenged the existing system, he did not campaign for a specific alternative.

In the Middle Ages the triangle was coordinated by social, political, and religious obligations, responsibilities, and rights that created a static social structure. This system appears like a stagnant dark age to those accustomed to rapid change and progress, but it did provide social stability for many centuries and had the support of the church.

Thus history proceeds from one perspective to another, always facing the same issues of scarcity and allocation. The answers come out in different ways, but Christians always desire to bridge the gap between the ancient and the modern in ways that fulfill the wishes of the Creator, the only constant in the long flow of history.

It is one thing to describe the different approaches to economic questions throughout history. It is quite another to explain why the differences occur. In order to answer this question, a brief look at four alternative worldviews is helpful. In a decidedly oversimplified form, the sketches on the next page depict four worldviews.

The first picture shows the ancient understanding that God, or the gods, created and controlled the universe. Like a great puppet master, God worked out his will on the landscape of the world on which people were placed. The ancient Hebrews were not the only people of their time to adopt this model. What differentiated them from others was that they had only one puppet master who pulled all the strings, and he had a desire for interaction and relationship with his people. Other people had many gods in charge of various aspects of life. Some embodied the deity as a ruler by divine right, whose command was absolute.

Figure 1.2
Worldviews

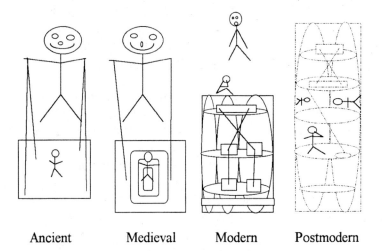

Ancient   Medieval   Modern   Postmodern

Obedience and loyalty were the appropriate policy or strategy for the subjects. In the case of Yahweh, a covenant relationship softened the arbitrary nature of God but did not change the basic understanding of how the world worked. The same pattern of authority and control was thought to be necessary in social structures and organization. People depended on their rulers to see that resources were sufficient. This comes through clearly in the story of Joseph and Pharaoh in Egypt as well as in other cases throughout the Bible. Chapter 3 will show Yahweh's plan for the provision of his people.

The Western medieval worldview was not much different from the ancient one except that social obligation and responsibility on the part of citizens was more elaborately defined, and the habits of God, the Western deity, followed consistent patterns understood as natural law. The four classifications of natural law by Thomas Aquinas illustrate the fact that the concept of natural law was little more than God's puppet strings programmed for his own convenience. The world still worked at God's command, and God maintained an interest in it. The sketch of the medieval worldview above removes some of the puppet strings, but it has orderly patterns on the world depicting the natural law of the scholastic. In economic life, the pattern of the feudal manor with rights and responsibilities for everyone became a kind of natural-law pattern of social organization.

The third sketch shows a Creator now detached from creation. The world is ordered by forces that function with the precision of a perpetual machine. Humanity is outside the machine, attempting to understand its workings through science. For economists, the person is both a student of and a part of the machine. People have regular patterns of behavior due to common goals and rational abilities, so social systems like resource allocation can be modeled just as well as systems of nature. The good life is attained by allowing the mechanisms to do their thing. In economics, the market is the mechanism, and a laissez-faire approach to policy is preferred. Science, not God, is king since science allows one to understand the mechanisms of the world. Also, pure science is value free since it merely unlocks the secrets of the way the world works. This worldview has been the guiding force of intellectual life during the last three or four centuries. We label ideas associated with this worldview "modernism." This worldview will be discussed further in chapter 10.

The fourth sketch attempts to show the current changes in thinking about how reality is perceived. The structures of the previous model are now dotted lines depicting the subjective and changing nature of what we believe is real, and the person is now a part of the system. The person's grasp of reality is conditioned by where one is in the scheme of things. What is a ceiling to one is a side wall to another, and the ceiling or wall has no standing on its own. This sketch is inadequate, but it does point toward the dynamic, subjective nature of reality in this worldview. In such a framework, terms like uniformity, regularity, and system-wide truths rarely apply. Relevant questions in this worldview might include the following. What is true for you? From what tradition do you come? Are there other perspectives that can enrich our view of this? One outcome of this approach is a world where all things are relative. No one can be sure what is absolutely true.

It took the church many decades to integrate the Enlightenment (modern) view of the world with historical Christianity. Some things, earlier considered wrong, now had to become acceptable. Examples include commercial activity, climbing a socioeconomic ladder, and charging interest. It will be even harder for Christians to deal with some of the ramifications of the postmodern world. Chapter 14 deals further with these challenges.

To summarize, the allocation and production concerns of life are addressed by working with the three sides of the economic context triangle. That effort is carried out under the rubric of a worldview that specifies the relevant questions and policies. Today we live in an environment where worldviews are changing, affecting both the economic and Christian understanding of what is true.

The next chapter explores sides 2 and 3 of this triangle to give a clearer perspective on the issues involved in production and consumption. These perspectives are relevant whether one has modern or postmodern leanings. Chapters 3-7 suggest an approach to the economic triangle that reflects kingdom-of-God values, which again are not tied to either one of the relevant worldviews. Chapters 8-11 explain how market capitalism deals with the economic triangle. These chapters represent the typical approach from a modern worldview. They describe the key concepts undergirding the capitalism we know today. Chapter 12 draws on the experience of Russia to illustrate that capitalism is far more than a technical system of allocation. In fact, it is part of a complex social fabric that is held together by a precarious social glue. Next, chapter 13 attempts to deal with issues that Christians face when economic thinking and Christian thinking conflict. Finally, in chapter 14, postmodernism is shown to be testing the foundations of modernism by claiming that economics is not a mechanistic tool. Instead, it is claimed to be a set of social institutions that are interdependent and unpredictable.

Discussion Questions

1. Is it true that people of all income levels and social structures feel a constant sense of shortage, whether of things or of time?
2. Is it a Christian virtue to be satisfied and stop striving for more?
3. From the brief description of modern and postmodern world-views, what challenges do you see for the Christian in each worldview?

2

Allocation of Resources

L et's continue the discussion of the economic triangle by exploring more fully the process of allocation for consumption in figure 1.1. Picture yourself as owner of a gas station in a town bracing for a hurricane. You have only one hundred gallons left in your supply tank, and ten cars are lined up, each needing fifteen gallons. You have an economic problem on your hands: you need a system to allocate the limited supply of fuel. What alternatives are available?

Deciding Who Gets What

First, you might use a *first-come, first-served* method. You could simply keep pumping until the seventh car exhausts the supply of gas. The remaining three cars get nothing. Whether the tenth car is an ambulance, or a police car, or driven by someone on their way to the hospital for emergency care, it will not be serviced. This first-come, first-served method places the highest value on being early. People with a low cost of time can afford to line up early for the fuel.

A second system might be to allocate resources based on *need*. In this case you would ask all drivers how they intended to use the gas and then decide, either by yourself or through a democratic process of voting or polling, how the gas should be divided. This system assumes that people have a generally accepted view of what need is and are prepared to live with the consequences of the allocation. Under this system, everyone has an incentive to appear most needy. If need is related to low income, there is incentive to be poor or at least to appear poor.

A third method of allocation is simply to give everyone in the line ten gallons of gasoline, irrespective of their place in line or their need. This system puts a high value on *equal treatment* of everyone, so there is no reason to be early in line or to project a position of need. But the system also faces difficulty in maintaining equality when, after serving one customer or more, someone new joins the line.

A fourth way of solving the problem is *cronyism*. In this system, the supplier identifies his regular customers or friends and gives them fuel. This gives people incentive to seek friendships with people of power and wealth. Political patronage and conformity to the wishes of those with resources characterize a system based on cronyism.

Another allocative process is *open conflict*. If the people waiting for gasoline became irate and feared losing their source of transportation, fights could erupt and the victor could have the fuel. This chaotic approach usually erupts when a society's institutional structures are so weak or unfair that people take matters into their own hands.

One other approach to resource allocation is the *auction* method, in which those who bid highest get the most gasoline. In this system, it is important to have enough money to bid to the level required to get the desired quantities of gasoline. Except for cases of inherited wealth or unmerited windfall income, one bids with money that comes from wages in the labor auction. Thus one's work effort is directly related to the amount of gas one can buy. This *link between allocation and production* is unique among all the methods discussed.

In any large economy, virtually every method described above is used formally or informally. However, in an overall economy, one method or another dominates economic exchange. In the United States, the auction method prevails. The fact that bidders and sellers exchange freely makes this method appealing to a

democratic tradition. In other parts of the world, where popula-
tions lack the sophistication and social support structures of low-
cost communication, information, transportation, and political
stability, the auction allocation mechanism works far less effectively. In societies with a tradition of centralized governmental
power or a dominant leader, a method that relies on the leader's
choices—what we described above as cronyism—is common.

No matter which system a society uses, it must deal with the
forces of supply and demand. If an auction isn't used, the people
who wait in line pay in money plus time rather than just money.
The king who allocates to his cronies pays in reduced political
support from the masses, who pay in reduced political and personal choice. In short, a price is paid whenever scarce resources
are allocated, though the effects differ depending on the method
used. We generally prefer a system that minimizes this cost.

Motivations to Produce

Because the consumption process is only one side of the economic triangle, we need to expand our discussion to include issues
related to production as well. Unfortunately, many Christians
consider economic systems only as consumption processes and
find the methods of allocation based on need and equality more
appealing than the auction method. The appeal of these methods
derives from biblical teaching that abhors extremes of wealth and
poverty and advocates an ethic of service to the poor as central to
the gospel. A relevant question might be, "Should Christian people operate with one allocative method in the community of faith
and another in dealing with the world at large?" Before we take
up that question in chapter 6, we need to gain further insight into
what makes an economic system work.

The output of goods and services that a society can produce
in any given time depends on the resources and technology available and on the worldview of the people. Before discussing the
technical, socioreligious, and natural factors involved in production, we need to consider incentives for people to produce. People

must have a reason to replace leisure with work if they are to produce goods and services. Incentives can come in at least three forms.

First is the *material* factor. Those who are rewarded for work with resources or money to buy resources, will work as long as they consider the rewards worth more than the leisure they give up. Since the auction or market system ties a person's standard of living to one's work effort, that system is ideal for societies that put top priority on high living standards. However, it is wrong to assume that other allocative systems have no material incentives to work. If a society produces only enough for subsistence, the alternative to work is starvation–a strong incentive to work even if the worker receives only a small share of the output.

A second motivation for work is the *social* and *psychological* benefit one derives from it. If work provides a creative outlet for one's abilities, and if one finds satisfaction in the group aspects of work, one can be highly productive regardless of whether payment is proportionate to output. Volunteers and people who accept less than they could earn elsewhere work because of this type of motivation. Recently retired people often feel the loss of these benefits after retirement until they find other outlets for creativity and service.

A third motivation might come from *political* pressure to produce. A system uses this motivation method when it requires specified amounts of output under threat of penalty or espouses production goals to which people willingly strive because they embrace its political goals.

All three of these motivations may be present simultaneously in any system, but usually one motivation dominates. The capitalistic Western world operates primarily on the belief that material rewards can keep productivity high. The social motivation is considered desirable but is viewed as weaker and is often traded away if material gains compete with social goals. In other words, people often reject meaningful and fulfilling but low-paying work to accept jobs that are less desirable except for the higher pay.

In short, capitalists believe that people behave as if they are motivated mainly by the prospect of material rewards. They believe any system that does not give full recognition to that fact will be doomed to low production, a low standard of living, and, therefore, an inferior existence.[1] Given this perspective, the only allocation and production mechanism that makes sense is the market price or auction system. To the capitalist, only this system can deliver the goods and preserve freedom.

One of the ironies of American capitalism is that, although it has fostered the notion that material reward is the primary reason for work, the material rewards to large numbers of people are declining. From 1977 to 1989, American personal real (adjusted for inflation) income increased by $740 billion, according to the Congressional Budget Office. Two-thirds of this increased real wealth went to the wealthiest 1 percent of the population. By 1989 that group's average annual income was $560,000. Meanwhile, the lower 40 percent of the population actually had their real incomes reduced during that twelve-year period.[2] If absolute and relative material standing is thought to be the most powerful incentive to work in American culture, it is small wonder that the jobs available to the lower 40 percent of the income earners are hard to fill with enthusiastic workers.

Critics of capitalism frequently hold a common view regarding the motivation to produce. They believe that people can move to a higher level of motivation than the goal for personal material reward. They emphasize social goals, arguing that people desire to contribute to the welfare of society and the common good in many areas. The willingness of people in developed countries to pay 50 percent or more of their income in taxes is an argument that people work for public interests as well as private returns. At the same time, there is ample evidence that tax rates can reach levels where the work effort is reduced and an economy deteriorates.

In any case, the Marxian or utopian notion that human nature is progressing toward a state where the masses will work toward an egalitarian common good is all but dead. The secular world seems unable to get beyond self-interest as a goal for work. Thus those countries that use free markets tend to generate higher average standards of living. Unfortunately, they do tend to have an increasing share of losers in the competitive fray, and this tendency is leading to increasingly costly social problems. In the secular world, the best that can be done is not always very good.

Christians, on the other hand, have more than their own material gain as a motivation to work. Scripture encourages work for material sufficiency, self-actualization, and social interaction, but it goes further. There are at least two additional motives for work. The first is the desire to serve those who need help by giving either income or labor. The second is the desire to use the workplace for witness and mission. Infiltrating the work environment for the cause of the gospel may not reform the world, but it can serve as salt and light to others and attract some to faith.

Indeed, these last two motivations should play a more important role in the believer's productive activity than the material rewards that dominate the work decisions of the majority of the population. The believer should not need a system driven by material benefits for high productivity.

Making Production Decisions

Once the motivation to produce is understood, it is necessary to explore what economists call the production function. Although this typically refers to the relationship between physical inputs and outputs, it is useful to broaden the scope of analysis to include both tangible and intangible inputs to and outputs from the process.

Tangible Factors in the Economy

Tangible inputs are easily listed: land, labor, capital, and entrepreneurship all are woven into a process that generates output. Any production effort must determine how these inputs are combined for maximum efficiency. This is an enormously complex problem because inputs often can substitute for each other. Assume a bushel of wheat could be produced on one hundred square feet of land with ten pounds of fertilizer, a mechanical robot, and one hour of human labor, or with one acre of land and one hundred hours of human labor. Which is better? The same question could be asked of alternative ways of teaching students, curing patients, making automobiles, or cutting hair.

The answer to this question is the economist's standard answer to most question: It all depends. It all depends on how plentiful or scarce the various resources are. If robots and fertilizer are hard to find but land is plentiful, the second way of growing wheat makes more sense than the first. Unfortunately, there are far more than two ways of growing wheat. In fact, millions of different combinations of the inputs could work. Deciding which is best is more difficult than it first appears.

Maybe the place to begin understanding production is with another question: Who should evaluate all the data to see which input allocations are best? This brings us to another set of alternatives similar to those we considered in the discussion of methods of allocation for consumption. First, we might appoint some group to be in charge of production, to research all the questions and answer them as best they can. By planning how much of all goods and services should be produced and the methods required to produce them, the group could attempt to steer society toward its goal. In addition, the planners would need to define, on the allocation side, what need and equality really mean. Good planners would listen closely to the wishes of the people so that the production and distribution questions were answered in socially desirable ways. If they failed, they might be fired—unless they had political power of dictatorial proportions, in which case only death or political revolution could remove them.

A second method of answering the production questions is the same auction environment discussed in the consumption section. Those with something to contribute to production offer it for sale if they choose to. People offer their labor. Mine owners offer their coal. Land owners offer land for sale or rent. People with extra funds offer them as loans to others who need extra money at the auction. As the auction proceeds, people listen to the auctioneer and alter their decisions in response to changing prices. For example, the journalist homemaker might seek a baby-sitter so that she would be free to enter the labor auction if the wage rate for journalists went high enough to attract her. People might adjust their spending and save more if the interest rate rose in the loanable funds market. Farmers might use less land and more fertilizer if land prices soared. These auctions are continuous and, in the process, people receive or lose income as they offer skills and resources for sale. Also, producers respond to price signals, choosing the collection of inputs available for production. In other words, it *all* depends on the prices of the inputs, which depend on the supply and demand of each resource in its respective auction.

If the production market is brought together with the allocation market, exchange activity goes on continuously with people receiving and spending money and reacting to market signals. All the while, the questions of what is produced, how it is produced, and who gets the production are being answered by the millions of decisions which buyers and sellers—consumers and producers—are making. This is the essence of a market economy. It sounds like a cumbersome process, but remember, the questions it is answering are extremely complex.

Intangible Factors in the Economy

The preceding discussion illustrates the tangible, technical side of production. Overlaying these technical considerations of production are the intangible issues of values, religion, ethics, and justice. Many studies show that these intangible factors heavily condition the technical outcomes.

For example, before the Reformation, the church taught against the desire to acquire riches. Later, during the Reformation, many secular occupations that had been viewed as spiritually inferior to church work became acceptable as callings from God.

The more communal focus of feudal lifestyles gave way to the elevation of individual pursuit. The desire to acquire and seek social advancement was no longer considered a sin, as the medieval world had seen it. Clearly, entrepreneurial economic activity gradually was becoming acceptable to God, at least from the viewpoint of the sixteenth-century Christian. One writer illustrates this well:

> The world of Today elbowed aside the world of Tomorrow, and as life on earth became more important, so did the notion of material standards and ordinary comforts. Behind the change in religious tolerance was the rise of Protestantism, which hastened a new attitude toward work and wealth.... Acquisitiveness became a recognized virtue–not immediately for one's private enjoyment, but for the greater glory of God. From here it was only a step to the identification of riches with spiritual excellence, and of rich men with saintly ones.[3]

Social customs as well as religious values sometimes constrain production behavior. Examples include biases against the employment of women or minorities that limit the efficiency of labor markets, a strong environmental consciousness that raises production costs, and community solidarity that slows down labor mobility.

In every society, the list of intangibles ultimately combines with technical factors to form the social fabric out of which an economic system is formed. It is a mistake to evaluate any economic system on the technical variables alone. Free-market outcomes may appear ideal to a capitalist in the United States. But they may seem wrong to members of the labor party in the Netherlands who are willing to trade some of their standard of living in order to adopt some economic planning that they believe will give jobs to more people. Since the fall of the Soviet Union, economists have been searching for ways to transplant markets to the fragmented former republics. Much of the frustration of that effort stems from differences in the intangibles of the Russian culture. That issue will be explored further in chapter 11.

Costs and Benefits of Managed Versus Free Markets

No system has markets that are either all managed or all free. Managed or planned production and allocation do occur in a free-exchange economy, and voluntary exchange exists in essentially managed economies. Thus the real problem is determining where managed markets stop and free markets begin.

Examples may be helpful here. In the home, family members don't bid for the food, clothing, and shelter available, and the tasks of production are usually planned in some sense. In general, parents are the central planners. They make decisions for the children, allocating resources according to some value system that, it is to be hoped, everyone perceives to be fair. Business enterprises, too, are usually centrally planned by the owners and managers so that complicated auction arrangements need not be set up for routine activities. In general, central planning is preferred when the costs of organizing effective auctions are greater than the benefits the markets bring to the participants.

The case of college class registration can be illustrative here. The University of Chicago Business School distributes coupons, pretend money, to its students each year. They can use the coupons to bid on classes they want to take. These coupons become bidding rights, a type of property right. The highest bidders get the class slots most in demand. Students must choose how to spend their coupons in ways that will bring them the most desired course schedules.

At Wheaton College, we allocate class slots differently. No auction exists. Students simply stand in line, and a first-come, first-served policy of allocation prevails. We impose a value system that says seniors get first place in the line and freshmen must go last. In the end, students seem to get the courses they want over a four-year period, but there is less of an auction environment and more of an administratively planned atmosphere. Both systems finally produce graduates, but with a differing selection process of course inputs.

Some time ago in a conversation with University of Chicago students and faculty who were discussing the bidding process, students were lamenting the fact that no futures market exists in coupons and that their freedom was therefore limited. After observing the energy spent on constructing the market environment of class registration, I commented that it might be much simpler to have a first-come, first-served method like most other schools use. One person responded that the value of freedom is high and needs to be protected at all costs.

The moral of this story is not that one side was for free markets and the other for managed markets. Rather, it was that I felt freedom by being released from the confusion of constructing and participating in registration markets, while they felt more freedom by being released from an imposed first-come, first-served system. No wonder families, firms, and countries prefer planning for some activities instead of the perpetual negotiating of a market environment. Markets are not costless. Some people prefer to avoid the cost of markets by sacrificing freedom in exchange for central organization.

But central planning is not costless either. As already mentioned, people who accept planning do sacrifice some freedom. They may also sacrifice efficiency. This is more obvious as the operation under consideration becomes larger and larger.

The manager of a small manufacturing company may efficiently plan the flow of labor, raw materials, and capital in this production process. But for someone to organize the flow of these resources throughout an entire society would be an enormous task requiring so much information as to be impossible at any cost. At some point it becomes apparent that markets can generate, collect, and process the required information through their pricing mechanism better than any planner. At that point markets become the appropriate mechanism to allocate the resources.

In general, the cost of the market process will be lower as people are better educated, vehicles for information flow are more developed, resources within a society are more mobile, and buyers and sellers are more numerous. This is especially so if these characteristics also lead toward independent thinking that resists the coercive aspects of planning.

Once again, the question for the Christian might be whether resource owners–including laborers–should be paid according to the market price signals of society or by some other method. The model developed in chapter 6 argues for market-resource pricing but makes a strong distinction between income and use of that income in consumption.

Conclusions: Freedom Versus Control

History shows that markets organize economic resources far better than planners.[4] The auction method of allocation provides such powerful incentives to produce that Western economists generally have disdained widescale central planning at the national level. For some, the efficiency question is at the heart of the discussion on managed versus free markets.

However, the more intense and emotional issue related to planning is the concern for freedom. At what point does one cross the line into oppression? Surely, children who resist the structure of parental authority are carrying freedom to the extreme. The students at the University of Chicago might build a compelling freedom case for auction registration, but few other students in the country have thought it important enough to seek changes in registration procedures. Only at more complex levels of resource organization is there more generalized consensus that planning is inevitably a serious threat to freedom. Chapter 10 will consider in more detail the appropriate role of government in a free economy.

The discussion so far has hinted that Christians follow a higher calling than do non-Christians, although few specifics have been developed. I have implied that Christians are to live in ways that point toward the coming kingdom of God and are to call the world around them toward a new life. The concepts of allocation and production in an environment of scarcity cannot be forgotten, but believers are called to handle these concerns in uniquely

Christian ways. The next five chapters explore the notion that believers must go beyond the best the secular world can do in economic life. They must model to the world a value system consistent with biblical teaching. This can be a powerful but largely untapped tool of evangelism for the kingdom of God.

Discussion Questions

1. Of all the methods of allocation, do some feel more Christian or less Christian than others? Why?
2. Is it true, as this chapter argues, that allocation systems cannot be evaluated purely on how Christian they appear to be, but also on how they structure production incentives?
3. Is it necessary for Christian people to have the material reward incentive in order to be productive, or is working a natural response to God's gift of resources and grace?
4. Illustrate, with examples from various cultures, the three motivations to work. Should others be added?
5. What do R. H. Tawney in *Religion and the Rise of Capitalism* and Max Weber in *The Protestant Ethic and the Spirit of Capitalism* add to the discussion on the role of religion in economic activity?
6. If optimal production-input combinations depend on the relative scarcity of the factors of production more than on the conclusions of intelligent engineers, what strategy for third-world economic development would you recommend?
7. Why might someone argue that auction class registration will lead to better classes than a first-come, first-served method?

3

Biblical Background to Economic Thinking

E conomic concerns are always prominent in the history of a people. Certainly this was true in Hebrew life as depicted in the Old Testament and in the Christian era of the New Testament. To be understood properly, Old Testament law must be studied in its theological and sociological setting. The Hebrew people of the ancient Near East were not just another group of nomads vying for the limited space of the Fertile Crescent. On the contrary, God had called them to a special task in history and had provided guidance to them in their mission. The guidance God provided has become source material for twentieth-century Christians, but it is not easy for us to understand and apply it.

Judaic law specified behavior in the context of a covenant relationship in which the people were required to maintain a specific social structure. In this structure the law made sense and could be applied meaningfully. Superimposing the behavioral part of the law on an alien social structure can lead to perverse outcomes.

For example, the social-welfare function of gleaning in the Hebrew system is more easily abused in an individual entrepreneurial environment than in a caring, community social structure. Millard Lind, in a paper on the economics of the Hebrews, refers to this process of applying Hebrew law to alien social environments as "cream skimming" maxims from the text.[1]

"Cream skimming" can occur when economists attempt to remove the Enlightenment philosophical underpinnings from contemporary democratic capitalism and replace them with selected features of Old Testament law.

For example, the suggestion that education for all is a modern application of the Jubilee principle (Lev. 25) has a certain appeal. However, if schools simply educate students in ways that do not reduce socioeconomic disparities, then the redistributive effects of education may be far less than hoped for. A substantial literature questions the redistributive effects of elementary and secondary education in the United States. It may be impossible to graft the Jubilee concept into American economic life as long as individual freedom and competition are fundamental to our social and economic organization. Social structure and theology come as a package and cannot easily be separated.[2]

A preferred approach is to come at the issue from the other direction. First, explore the social structure that is most suited to the entire biblical record, and then examine how we might change the social structure to conform more closely to the teachings of Scripture. To proceed in this venture, we must first recognize that the law came to a theocratic society through which God had chosen to work out his unique purposes. The counterpart in our contemporary world is the church, not any secular state or social group. Therefore, the biblical content speaks first to the church, and a Christian economics must reflect the kind of economic relationships and behavior that is normative for believers as a body.

Biblical Norms and Counterculture

The claim that social structures condition behavior does not mean that a community of faith must have a social structure like that of the people of God in Bible times if it is to be faithful to Scripture. Rather, it means that social organization among believers must have characteristics compatible with the core teaching in Scripture on economic relationships, even if the surrounding society accepts another kind of social pattern. This two-kingdom view of God's work in the world will be developed later, but it is important to emphasize here that this approach views God as working on two fronts in creation and sees the church as having a special place in his plans.

Certainly all of creation is God's domain and ultimately serves his purposes. Nevertheless, God has selected those who come to faith as special witnesses to the radical calling that brings him special glory. The biblical record reveals that calling and shows how faithfulness to it is the best evangelistic message to the secular world. We shortchange the message of the gospel and the witness of the church when we start from any secular social and economic system and attempt to leaven it with a piecemeal application of biblical principles while ignoring the far-reaching social implications of the Scripture. Ultimately, believers are aliens and strangers in the secular world; their involvement with it is like that of travelers in a foreign land. Obviously they must interact with the secular system, but their focus is on the new life that cannot be understood by unbelievers unless they come to faith.

The social and economic system of the Hebrews differed dramatically from anything around them. The Egyptian monarchy and the city-states of Palestine were highly centralized in structure. Excessive service and wealth were given to royalty. Slavery and class distinctions were the norm, and power and violent force were the tools of social order. A weak king and ineffective military meant almost certain social chaos or takeover by an outside power. Lesser nations sought, through alliances or tribute payments, to maintain autonomy as long as possible, but loyalty to agreements meant little when alternative opportunity appeared. Income distribution was unequal by design. Challenging this way of doing things made little sense since no alternatives seemed practical.

Into this world, God called a people and presented them with values that seemed hopelessly radical. First, there was to be no king. The entire pyramid of power was inverted so that the household, rather than the royalty, became the focus of attention. The family, clan, tribe, and nation were designed to support the household in all affairs of life. Figure 3.1 illustrates the way in which the social structure was put together.

Figure 3.1
Hebrew Social Structure

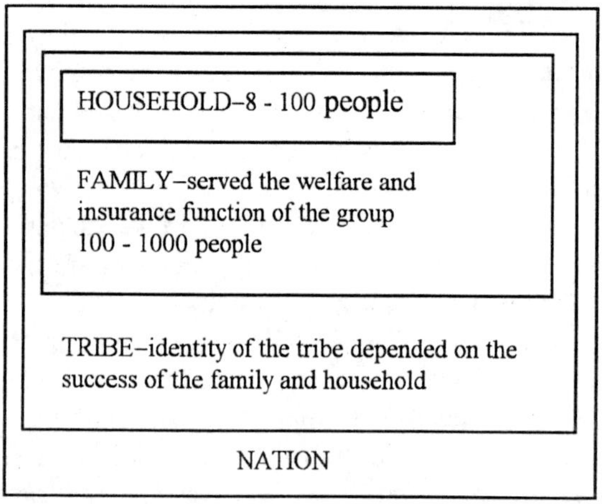

HOUSEHOLD–8 - 100 people

FAMILY–served the welfare and
insurance function of the group
100 - 1000 people

TRIBE–identity of the tribe depended on the
success of the family and household

NATION

The social structure had the larger units serving the smaller units rather than the usual reverse pattern.

Alternative models were employed by the Hebrews throughout their history. The exodus and wilderness experiences were clearly more nomadic than the picture of Hebrew life presented here. Likewise, God did not reject the reign of the kings. However, the wanderings and the royalty experiences were aberrations from God's design for his people. This view is shown in the prophetic critique of kingship found in Deuteronomy 17 and 1 Samuel 8-10, and in the fact that much of the wilderness experience was punishment rather than part of the ideal plan.

Perhaps the book of Ruth is the most beautiful example of how this social system was supposed to work. Naomi and her family left Judah during a famine and took up residence in Moab, a neighboring country. There Naomi's husband and two sons died, leaving her with two Moabite daughters-in-law, one of whom, Ruth, returned to Judah with her. Then the family or clan of Naomi's deceased husband began the process of restoring Naomi into the system by applying norms of the Mosaic law.

The process began with Ruth's gleaning and ended with Boaz's purchase of Naomi's land and marriage to Ruth. At the birth of Ruth's first son, the process of being restored to the fold of Israel was complete. The social system had worked, as witnessed by Naomi's friends, who said, "Praise be to the Lord, who this day has not left you without a kinsman-redeemer" (Ruth 4:14, NIV). It is no accident that the term used for kinsman-redeemer in this Hebrew text is parallel to the Greek word for ransom, used to describe the redemptive work of Christ in Mark 10:45. God wants social structures to protect against destitution and alienation. A decentralized web of mutual responsibility and accountability among all groupings of society was God's design for his people, rather than the top-down, royalty-to-serf structure of Israel's contemporaries or the individualized responsibility and accountability of our modern Western world.

In many respects, God's intentions for his people were radically countercultural, and his covenant with the Hebrews required that they be faithful to his expectations if they were to receive his blessing and protection. The Hebrews' repeated unfaithfulness is not surprising in view of the radical nature of God's wishes. Thus the constant refrain of Scripture tells how God was calling his people back to himself and his ways. From Genesis to Revelation, we read of God's people following other gods and of God calling them back through prophets, preachers, and circumstances. Throughout history, God continues to call his people back to practices that seem utopian to anyone heavily involved in the world. The Old Testament documents that the Hebrews never were able to free themselves from the desire to be like others. This book develops the thesis that such a desire is a timeless temptation, nearly impossible to resist without a supporting community of faith.

While the Old Testament prophets strongly criticized patterns of behavior that broke down the web of protection against poverty, they do not appear to have indicted generalized prosperity. The Old Testament is full of examples of God blessing his people materially. In these cases, however, there is an underlying confidence that, if the law is kept, the social structure will filter out the dangers of wealth accumulation. Boaz was wealthy, but he used his wealth to carry out the intent of the law. The same is true of many Old Testament persons, although the temptations of wealth and power were too great for some, such as Solomon.

Later Jewish Teaching

Jewish teaching since Old Testament times has sought to condition economic behavior through the use of legal codes, communal legislation, and religious literature. No economic system is endorsed or condemned in Judaic teaching. However, there is a clear expectation that all systems should conform to religious constraints. Meir Tamari, in *With All Your Possessions,* describes limitations that Judaism places on economic activity.

1. There is a limitation on the time allowed for economic activity, because of the obligation to study Torah.

2. The production or sale of goods or services that are harmful to their consumers, either physically or morally, is forbidden.

3. One is responsible for damages caused by one's body or property.

4. Theft or economic dishonesty in any form or guise is forbidden

5. One is required to limit one's appetite for material goods. One's disposable income is also automatically reduced by the demands of *tsedakah* (social welfare) and interest-free loans, and by taxation to finance welfare, education, and the physical well-being of the community.[3]

The specific directives relating to these limitations make it clear that religious concerns were of first importance in Jewish teaching over the centuries. One example of how this teaching affected behavior can be seen in the first limitation. Since any time spent in economic life detracted from study of the Torah, there is a bias against occupations that do not have considerable flex-time built in. Consequently, a recurring theme in Jewish teaching encourages commerce rather than farming as an occupation because commerce allows more time for religious study.[4]

The Messianic Mission of Jesus

By the time the New Testament writers came on the scene, a great deal had changed. The concept of Israel as an eminent, politically autonomous power or minipower had faded for all but the Zealots. The Romans, though outwardly detested by most of their subjects, had brought considerable political stability to the Mediterranean world and allowed limited governing rights to local groups under their control. Within Israel, the hope for the promised Messiah was still nurtured, and that hope was cast in terms of a political resurgence, but few saw any simple divine escape from Rome.

Into this climate came John the Baptist and then Jesus with a strange and confusing message. Jesus' message was so unusual that the devil tried to sidetrack him into a more conventional messianic strategy. After Jesus was baptized, he went into the wilderness. There he fought off the temptation to carry out the messianic responsibilities in economic, political, and established religious ways (Matt. 4; Luke 4). When he began to pursue the suffering-servant way of the cross, the alienation process began that led to Calvary and death. Apart from the resurrection, Jesus is little more than a wise teacher with some unique powers. But the resurrection did occur, and thus the story of God's work in the world goes on.[5]

Jesus, to the disappointment of many, did not speak of the kingdom of God as a theocracy of the Jews. In fact, he rarely discussed politics in a direct sense. For him, the kingdom of God was a way of life for believers in community.

What this means for the economic relationships of believers in the modern world is the next topic of the book. We will look at it in three parts: The first deals with the movement of the work of God from the theocracy of Israel to the believers church. The second interprets New Testament passages on wealth and income in light of the modern capital-oriented market economy. The third sketches what economic relationships among believers ought to be like.

The law of Moses looked forward to something more inclusive and complete, something Jesus called the kingdom of God. In Christ, God's plan for people came to fruition. His effort to communicate the significance of God's kingdom became the major part of his ministry. The establishment of the church was an important step in fleshing out that kingdom in the world.

Discussion Questions

1. Do you agree with Lind's assessment that Christians have tried to "cream skim" maxims out of Scripture and ignored the implications of the text on social structures? Support your answer with examples.

2. Is it appropriate to use a social structure designed for a theocracy as a model for a secular social environment? If so, give examples where such a process has been successful. If not, is the biblical theocratic model applicable to the church today, or is it completely irrelevant in modern times?

3. Is it possible that an application of the social principles of the Hebrews, if applied by the community of believers today, would be a form of witness and evangelism?

4. Could you outline a few points for a research paper on how the church related biblical teaching to social structures throughout the Middle Ages? Ideally, this history would be an important and lengthy addition to this chapter.

4

The Two-Kingdom Approach to the Bible

One of the most exciting and frightening realizations that comes from a casual reading of the New Testament is that the kingdom of God was already being established, in part, on earth in the first century. Matthew 12:28 associates Christ's casting out of demons with the coming of the kingdom, suggesting that it had already broken through and was seeking citizens willing to identify with it. That God had broken directly into history and was building the kingdom is exciting, but a more penetrating look at the kind of kingdom he was building is frightening. The kingdom demands a high level of commitment from the believer. In the New Testament, the terms *kingdom of God* and *kingdom of heaven* are used synonymously, and together the passages form a composite that is worthy of careful attention from all Christians. Theologians from early Christianity to the present have struggled with the meaning of the term *kingdom of God*. It is called

> the sovereignty, reign, or rule of God.... The basic message of Jesus (Matt. 4:17; Mark 1:15) and his disciples (Matt. 10:7; Luke 10:9,11) was that the Kingdom of God had come near.... When it came, God's will would be done on earth (Matt. 6:10). Only those who, in the meantime, lived in accordance with God's will might hope to enter it (Matt. 5:3-10; 7:21-23).... Nevertheless, ... Jesus believed the Kingdom of God was already present in some way: in his person, as the one who would be Messiah in the coming king-

45

dom, in his power to [cast out] demons, or ... in the response of
faith by those who repented and changed their lives.[1]

Questions arise because there seems to be a progressive sense
in which the reign of Christ is fulfilled. The present and future
characteristics of the kingdom have been interpreted differently
over the centuries, and many do not agree on the distinctions between the Christian and the secular in modern history.

The preceding definition emphasizes the powerful reign of
God through Christ, the Messiah. This rule often is broadened to
include the secular and the sacred, and it points toward the future
in a powerful way, predicting that the secular will be overcome by
the sacred. The definition also focuses on the group of believers
who are committed to God's rule and live as a body of the redeemed in the present. This emphasis is more temporal for those
who live in the kingdom, and it involves a struggle against the
secular world, which seeks to establish a kingdom of its own (1
John 5:19).

The approach taken in this book focuses on the second of
these two emphases. Our main concerns are the differences between the two worlds and the responsibilities of believers as citizens of the kingdom of God in economic matters. A corollary
concern is that in economic life, contemporary evangelicals have
lost the distinction between the two kingdoms.

The Characteristics of the Kingdom

It is appropriate to review some prominent characteristics that
will identify the kingdom of God in our time. First, the story of
Nicodemus hints at the radical nature of the calling into the kingdom. Jesus comments that "no one can see the kingdom of God
without being born from above" (John 3:3). For Nicodemus, who
was taught the mind-set of the Pharisees, only a new orientation, a
new mind-set, a new worldview, could help him see the kingdom.
The change is so dramatic that it requires a new history for mind
and heart.

The new birth of which Jesus spoke is equally important today because of the secular mind-set that is so pervasive in our
time. Only a new worldview can free one from the power of the
world's mold. Therefore, a primary requirement for the kingdom
of God today is a new birth of the mind and heart that will foster
a careful approach to secular ideals and values.

A second characteristic of the kingdom is illustrated in the
parable of the sower in Matthew 13, where Jesus indicates that
citizenship in God's kingdom is given only to those who overcome
the significant odds of temptation, superficial commitment, and
attachment to the secular preoccupations of success and security.
Only those who remain good soil and bear fruit are worthy of the
kingdom.

> Hear then the parable of the sower. When anyone hears the word
> of the kingdom and does not understand it, the evil one comes and
> snatches away what is sown in the heart. This is what was sown
> on the path. As for what was sown on rocky ground, this is the
> one who hears the word and immediately receives it with joy; yet
> such a person has no root, but endures only for a while, and when
> trouble and persecution arises on account of the word, that person
> immediately falls away. As for what was sown among thorns, this
> is the one who hears the word, but the cares of the world and the
> lure of wealth choke the word, and it yields nothing. But as for
> what was sown on good soil, this is the one who hears the word
> and understands it, who indeed bears fruit and yields, in one case
> a hundredfold, in another sixty, and in another thirty. (Matt.
> 13:18-23)

A third characteristic of the kingdom is that its citizens exist
in society alongside citizens of the secular kingdom. They are not
isolated or separate from the world geographically. The parable of
the wheat and the weeds in Matthew 13:24-30 indicates that,
though the two kingdoms are clearly distinguishable, they coexist
in society. Christians are in the world but do not belong to the
world (John 17:11, 14, 16). What it means to "not belong to the
world" is one of the more ignored themes in Scripture because

contemporary Christianity in the west has strongly identified with this world and does not have a countercultural approach to life in the world. On this topic Ronald J. Sider wrote:

> Two Biblical texts serve well to underline my thesis. The first is Matthew 7:13, "Enter by the narrow gate for the gate is wide and the way is easy, that leads to destruction and those who enter by it are many." And the second is Romans 12:1, 2, "I appeal to you therefore, siblings, by the mercies of God, to present your bodies as a living sacrifice, holy and acceptable to God, which is your spiritual worship. Do not be conformed to this world but be transformed by the renewal of your mind, that you may prove what is the will of God, what is good and acceptable and perfect."
>
> Too many Christian colleges have forgotten the very sharp contrast the New Testament draws between the church and the world. Jesus stated bluntly that the world "hates me because I testify of it that its works are evil" (John 7:7)....
>
> The church and the world are in deadly conflict. Many Christian colleges refuse to accept the depth and breadth of that conflict. Yet the fundamental incompatibility between the world and Jesus' new community is so great that 1 John says we cannot love the world and the Father at the same time: "Do not love the world or the things of the world. If you love the world, the love for the Father is not in you. For all that is in the world, the lust of the flesh, and the lust of the eyes, and the pride of life, is not of the Father but is of the world" (1 John 2:15-16).[2]

Although Sider's message is directed to the Christian college, he points out that the true kingdom of God contrasts dramatically with the secular kingdom in which it lives. One may suggest that the Judeo-Christian influence on Western culture and the Enlightenment view of humanity has reduced the hostility of society toward the kingdom of God. But it takes considerable imagination to believe that the approach to life of the secular kingdom has become more compatible with the teachings of Jesus.

Matthew 13:44-48 claims that the kingdom of heaven is worth more to the believer than all the secular kingdom has to offer. At Jesus' trial he made it clear that the source of his kingdom is different from the secular kingdom's origin and that his kingdom therefore operates by different behavioral norms. "My kingdom is not from this world. If my kingdom were from this world, my followers would be fighting to keep me from being handed over to the Jews. But as it is, my kingdom is not from here" (John 18:36).

The characteristics of the kingdom listed so far are significant, but they do not give clear behavioral direction to citizens of the kingdom. On issues of behavioral norms, ambiguity occurs in the Christian experience. This is particularly true in economic life, where Christians reach virtually no consensus on norms for economic behavior.

The lack of consensus among believers on economic concerns arises because much of the biblical content on economic behavior appears obscure or idealistic. Believers often feel as if they must fall back on secular norms as guidelines for economic behavior because the Bible's answers just don't seem applicable. Hence, to develop an appropriate strategy for the Christian, let us examine two more significant and related characteristics of the kingdom of God.

First, those who share in the fellowship of faith have a special responsibility to *discern* right and wrong in many controversial matters. The fact that wisdom is imparted through the group, not through individuals alone, is a prominent theme in the New Testament. This is not to suggest that the word from the Lord cannot come to individuals. It merely recognizes that in many difficult and controversial issues, there are ambiguities. In such cases, group discernment and discipling are necessary. Even when an individual claims to have a word from the Lord, the validity of that claim frequently is tested by the group, which has a broader base of spiritual gifts.

The effectiveness of the group in decision-making and ministry derives from the way in which God has endowed the community of faith with an assortment of gifts. The body of believers is compared in Scripture with the human body. Individuals complement and support each other with their respective gifts (1 Cor. 12:4-7; Rom. 12:6). These gifts are given for the common good and work together to help the body discern its direction with wisdom. Sharing, rejoicing, weeping, and praying with each other, as a closely knit family would do, are also essential characteristics of Christians (Rom. 12:10-13). Perhaps 1 Corinthians 13 is the key to the success of the body of believers in the world. If the church can express *agape* love within itself in the manner described in this passage, then the other characteristics of the kingdom will become by-products of that expression. Thus the discerning function of the church will be practiced more faithfully.

Second, because believers have been bonded together with complementary gifts that help them to discern what should be done, they also are charged with the responsibility to *disciple* each other so that they can remain faithful to their calling. The care with which Jesus built the church indicates how important the body of believers was to him. The work of discipling was one task to which he paid special attention. His response when Peter affirmed that Jesus was the Christ (Matt. 16:16) indicates that the church, as a body of believers, was to play an important role in discipling those who were committed to the kingdom of God. An example of how this discipling or "binding and loosing" process is to function appears in Matthew 18:15-20. In this case a person is instructed to resolve conflict by moving progressively toward more involvement with fellow church people until a solution is found. Thus in matters of discipling, Jesus has given the church substantial power to forbid or permit certain conduct. Jesus reinforces this concept in John 20:23 by giving the disciples the power to forgive sins.

Jesus' further statement to Peter in Matthew 16:17-19 helps to clarify this issue. D. A. Carson, in *The Expositor's Bible Commentary*, points out that the keys to the kingdom and the responsibilities of binding and loosing spoken of in these verses belong to the committed believers who are mainstream in the secular world.

In full Christian perspective the kingdom will be consummated in sudden, apocalyptic fashion at the Parousia, when God's actions are final and quite independent of human means. But now the keys of the kingdom are confided to [people]. They must proclaim the Good News, forbid entrance, urge conversion. They constitute a small minority in a big world: their mission will be to function as the eschatological *ekklesia,* the people of God Jesus is building within this world. Inevitably the assignment involves them in using the keys to bind and loose. These verses are therefore the result of the partially realized and one day to be consummated eschatology implicit in the New Testament.[3]

The point of this interpretation is that, although Peter did play a special role in church history, the body of believers as a called-out church has responsibility to use the keys of the kingdom. Carson continues:

Confirmation that this is the way 16:19 is to be taken comes at 18:18. If the church, Messiah's eschatological people already gathered now, has to exercise the ministry of the keys, if it must bind and loose, then clearly one aspect of that will be the discipline of those who profess to constitute it. Thus the two passages are tightly joined: 18:18 is a special application of 16:19. Again, if we may judge from Paul's ministry, this discipline is a special function of apostles, but also of elders and even of the whole church (1 Cor. 5:1-13; 2 Cor. 13:10; Titus 2:15; 3:10-11)–an inescapable part of following Jesus during this age of the inaugurated kingdom and of the proleptic gathering of Messiah's people. The church of Jesus Christ is more than an audience.... The continuity depends as much on discipline as on truth. Indeed, faithful promulgation of the latter both entails and presupposes the former.[4]

Howard A. Snyder, in The *Community of the King,* also speaks of the church as the body that gives substance to the kingdom of God in our time. "The Kingdom of God has not fully come but it is coming. Its full establishment awaits the return of Christ. But through the life and work of God's people–the

Church–it continues to expand and grow. And understanding the Kingdom is closely bound up with understanding the Church."[5]

The Contrast of the Kingdoms

Thus, to summarize, the kingdom of God, as personified in the community of faith, contrasts sharply with the secular kingdom in which that community lives. Active participation in it is required of the Christian, and the community's sincere efforts to find truth and encourage people to practice it will be rewarded if members are committed enough to love each other and work together as a body.

This two-kingdom model in no way denies the universality of God's domain. It merely recognizes that part of that domain although under his control has not committed itself to his highest purpose. Further, the kingdom of God is not fully here because people are frail and come short of God's ideal even in their best moments. Yet, believers are to "strive first for the kingdom of God and his righteousness" (Matt. 6:33) and, with God's help, are able to have glimpses of how God wants the redeemed to live.

The preceding discussion is shown schematically below.

Figure 4.1
The Two Kingdoms

Kingdom of God (A)		Kingdom of this World (B)
• Inhabited by those who, by God's grace, are made whole and bear fruit	→	• Inhabited by those who have not accepted God's remedy for sin
• Clearly distinguished from secular society		• Self-centered, seeking to gratify desires
• Has a unique source (not from this world)	(C)	• Right and wrong determined by influential and powerful people
• Has the power of discerning right and wrong in ambiguous situations		• Functions in an atomistic, individualistic mode
• Functions as a community of interrelated parts	←	• Temporal only
• Temporal and eternal		

In this case the secular kingdom relates to the Western market capitalistic orientation. The two kingdoms are depicted as mutually exclusive because of the differences in their origin, goals, and philosophical orientation. Obvious areas of meaningful overlap will be discussed later, but for now the differences are our primary concern.

From figure 4.1, three areas of discussion can be identified. The first concern is about the relationships within the kingdom of God. These relationships are labeled *A* in the figure. Scripture has much to say about the interactions among believers in all areas of life, but only the economic relationships will be explored in the following chapters.

Letter *B* identifies relationships in secular society. In the economic area, these vary depending on the particular economic system accepted by a given society. As a rule, these relationships serve the interests of whatever social unit secular society considers most important. In some cases, as in Western capitalism, the basic social unit is the individual; in other cases, the state is foremost. Scripture says little about these relationships except for a few reality statements about the secular kingdom's economic situation.

Letter *C* stands for the interkingdom relationships. How does the Christian relate to the economic institutions of the secular environment? This question will be addressed in chapter 12, following closer examination of the intrakingdom relationships depicted in *A* and *B*.

Figure 4.2 can be a useful framework for further discussion because there can be a great deal of confusion in the interpretation of biblical passages if those that refer to one set of relationships are applied to another. For example, the type of sharing expected of believers cannot be expected of unbelievers, who are not committed to the discipline of a community of faith. Likewise, it is unlikely that the secular world can operate with the economic norms the church should practice.

Figure 4.2
Comparison of the Kingdoms

Kingdom of God (A)	(C)	Kingdom of this World (B)
• The total welfare of people	key goal	• Individual freedom symbolized in the right of private property
• Christian love	motivating to reach goal	• Self-interest with some moral restraints
• Cooperation	means to goal	• Competition
• Need-based voluntary sharing	allocative device	• Auction price system
• Church involvement in norm setting and discipling	regulator or guide over process	• Limited government

The two-kingdom model becomes more meaningful when realistically illustrated. Using democratic capitalism as representative of a given secular system, and the New Testament teachings as representative of the qualities of the kingdom of God, one can draw a series of contrasts. Figure 4.2 depicts the economic subset of figure 4.1. Oversimplification can easily occur in this kind of description of the two systems. However, there is enough contrast between them to make this dichotomy a useful tool for analysis.

Although there are, perhaps, as many different sets of secular economic characteristics as there are systems, the constant in the discussion is that secular systems all contrast sharply with the qualities of the kingdom of God. Thus Christians will always feel a tension in economic behavior. Indeed, they should always feel like pilgrims and strangers when immersed in the institutions of the secular world. However, for the most part, Western Christians do not feel that way. Many believe that a little fine-tuning of secular economic relationships can make them consistent with kingdom-of-God norms.

The Community of Faith and Kingdom Practice

At this point a question frequently arises. What types of organizations can be expected to operate with kingdom-of-God norms? Are Christian colleges, parachurch organizations, and large congregations expected to function with the kingdom-of-God relationships? They probably are not in terms of process, but they should reflect the outcomes that smaller communities of faith generate. In a college of several thousand people, it may be impractical to base salaries directly on need. However, every believer should be part of some community of faith that seeks to practice kingdom-of-God values in a caring environment with discipling and accountability. Need would then be addressed in these settings. Self-actualization and security for persons and their families should be part of the setting where the kingdom of God is becoming a reality.

The institutional framework most helpful in meeting these characteristics seems to have the following qualities:

1. The community of faith must be small enough that all members can share in a committed and caring way with each other (perhaps five to ten families).

2. Each community of faith should be part of a larger body that can offer general counsel and support and perhaps be a context for worship. This may be a larger congregation or a conference body that offers programs that a small group cannot provide. Christian education, mission outreach programs, publishing capability, and help in determining general behavioral norms are functions that the small community of faith might seek from the larger congregation or district group.

3. A denominational tie is valuable for a worldwide witness and a theological and historical heritage. Internationalizing the Christian vision is essential to prevent a community of faith from becoming ingrown and provincial.

Thus the community of faith will most likely be a small subset of a larger congregation that has denominational ties. The collection of all true believers everywhere constitutes the whole church that is attempting to help practice the ideals God gives his people. The model of those ideals toward which the church is striving is the kingdom of God, a reality that is breaking through even now.

Two things remain to be done in fleshing out kingdom-of-God relationships. First, we must solve the hermeneutical problem of how the economist of a modern capitalist society should read biblical literature, which is totally precapitalist in orientation. Second, we need to paint a picture of what some intra kingdom-of God relationships might look like in our time.

Discussion Questions

1. Do you think that this two-kingdom approach to the application of biblical principles underestimates the potential for good done by the secular world?
2. This two-kingdom approach implies that believers have a higher calling and different behavioral expectations for themselves than for nonbelievers. Do you believe this is appropriate? If so, what implications might this have for social and political behavior as well as economic practice?
3. Can you articulate the arguments of those like George Gilder, in *Wealth and Poverty*, and Michael Novak, in *The Spirit of Democratic Capitalism*, who suggest that the Christian tradition and market capitalism share the same values?

5

Reading the Bible With Modern Glasses

From our perspective, people in Bible times held two strange ideas about economic activity. First, they thought there were only so many goods and services available to be distributed to the people. Their thinking did not include increasing the economic pie by expanding productivity over time. Second, they thought this constant pie of production was fixed permanently at roughly an amount equal to what it took to keep the population alive and well but not expanding. In other words, life was destined to be a subsistence, steady-state existence.

There was natural productivity in nature, to be sure. Seeds grew into plants with many seeds, and people could more than replace themselves with large families, as could animals. But the trend was not toward growth, because natural productivity barely kept ahead of subsistence needs. Crops were consumed as fast as they were produced; death rates and birth rates were similar from year to year; famine, plague, and war constantly threatened the survival of the human race.

Nevertheless, prosperity is mentioned frequently in Scripture. Many refer to the Old Testament passages where obedience led to plenty (Deut. 8:12-20;1 Kings 10). Others see economic growth assumed in the teachings of Paul or the parables of Jesus (Eph. 4:28; Luke 12:1-21). However, there is a difference between the ability to work hard, produce, and even prosper for a time; and on

57

the other hand the concept that higher and higher living standards will prevail because of perpetual technology-driven growth. The ancient world saw prosperity as an unusual favor from God or the gods: a return for obedience that could be quickly lost. In the mind of the Western capitalist, growth comes from the productivity of capital and high savings rates and is expected as the normal pattern. In the ancient worldview, God gives the increase; in the modern world, the increase comes as people fit into the normal pattern of how the world works. The ancient view was confirmed by the perpetually low standard of living experienced by the average citizen of the time. The modern view is confirmed by the long-run trend toward increasing living standards of successive generations over several centuries.

From the earliest estimates up to the fifteenth century, the size of the earth's population increased only slightly by modern standards, and the standard of living was rarely much above subsistence. In fact, it was news when someone prospered for a time. In Old Testament times, Jacob returned wealthy to his homeland from Laban's town, but later he became dependent on Egypt's bounty for subsistence. In this case as for Abraham and others, wealth was mainly in the form of cattle, sheep, and goats. Precious metal was a component of wealth, but it was usually in the form of jewelry of some kind. Not until the seventh century B.C. did coins appear as a medium of exchange or store of value. The earliest known Hebrew coin was minted in Judah in the fifth century B.C.[1] Whatever the form of wealth, it was seen not as a ticket to perpetual prosperity but as a reprieve from the hardships of nature or a display of power and influence. The display of wealth by the Hebrew kings was evidence of their power and influence in domestic and foreign relationships, but the prophets also viewed it as a cause of poverty in the land. One author describes precapitalist wealth as follows:

> Wealth appears in such forms as goods or services devoted to luxury consumption, to the maintenance and deployment of armed force, to religious edifices, or simply to display. Wealth thereby

takes on the properties of "use values," to use the term that Marx adopts from Adam Smith and Aristotle, including not least the use value of expressing the might and grandeur of rulership itself.

Conspicuously absent from these means of utilizing wealth is its application for a purpose central to, and indeed constitutive of, capitalism. This is the use of wealth in various concrete forms, not as an end in itself, but as a means for gathering more wealth. The closest analogue to this in ancient kingdoms, is the employment of military or religious or regal institutions and equipages, not merely as symbols of power and prestige desired for their own sakes but as instruments for military, religious, or dynastic expansion.[2]

The important part of all of this discussion is that precapitalist societies had no understanding of the economic-growth-and-prosperity mentality of the twentieth-century capitalist. Conversely, the modern capitalist finds it difficult to step into the shoes of the first-century farmer or craftsman. Consequently, we read into Scripture things that are not there, and we miss some of the lessons that are being taught.

This gulf of misunderstanding has contributed much to a widespread misreading of biblical texts on wealth. The thesis of this chapter is that the biblical writers had little if any perspective on productive capital as a form of wealth; Scripture therefore is silent on that recent form of wealth.[3] Instead, wealth was viewed as hoarded future consumption that contributed nothing to future production.

The biblical world saw three uses for income. First, everyone used part of present income for present consumption. Maintaining a certain standard of living was an important claim on income. Second, part of income went to tithes and offerings. Third, people saved for future consumption. This last category was particularly difficult to justify because, in a world where subsistence living was common, there were always poor people whose income had fallen below their basic needs.

The statement "You always have the poor with you" (John 12:8) can best be understood in light of this static subsistence type of thinking. It would be incorrect to assume that the same statement must apply to a machine-oriented, growth economy that is above subsistence level in per capita income.

It is also important to recognize that this no-growth subsistence orientation to economic life leads naturally to strong admonitions against accumulated wealth and to a concentrated focus on income distribution questions rather than production questions. If accumulated wealth was primarily a storing process for future consumption while others were starving, it is not surprising that so many biblical writers clearly spoke against accumulated wealth and emphasized sharing with the poor.

Jesus' parable in Luke 12:13-21 illustrates this thinking well. A farmer with large crops built bigger barns to house his harvest for future consumption. Apparently his savings helped no one in the present. Jesus condemned as sinful and foolish this practice of securing one's future rather than giving to the poor. Immediately after telling this parable, Jesus taught about curbing both consumption and savings, concluding in verse 33 by urging his listeners to divest themselves of their hoarded savings by giving to the poor. This directive fits well with the notion that earthly things decay, rust, and become depleted rather than expand, reproduce, and lead to growth for the good of society.

The principle that comes through again and again is that it is wrong to secure your future materially while others are starving. Wealth in Bible times was little more than hoarded resources that prevented others from consuming. It added nothing to future production. Since the pie of production was considered fixed near a subsistence level, accumulated wealth practically guaranteed that some people would be poor.[4]

The task for believers today is to distinguish the productive-capital-oriented wealth of the modern economy from the hoarded-wealth passages of the biblical texts. Two elements of this task are important. First, we must understand the nature of productive capital and prove that productive capital was not part of the understanding of biblical writers. Second, we must develop the implications of this analysis for a modern understanding of the anti-wealth passages of Scripture.

Viewing Wealth as Productive Capital Is a New Idea

The idea is quite new that inventions and creations of people could multiply the output of goods and services, resulting in persistent economic growth and an elevated standard of living. Not until after A.D. 1000 did capital inventions and innovative processes begin to expand production in ways that caused some to think of continued growth as a possibility. Between A.D. 1000 and 1500 the three-field system dramatically increased agricultural output; the four-wheeled wagon was invented; horses replaced oxen as field animals, reducing the number of people required for field work; and the enclosure movement of land ownership transformed common property into private property. These innovations brought amazing results, but they were only a foretaste of the increased output that would come in the industrial revolution of the eighteenth century.[5] The unleashing of productive forces in that century forever changed the way people think about resources and production.

The change was not just technical. Attitudes toward growth, acquisition, education, and social order changed radically. The following quote represents not only medieval thought but also thinking that had prevailed for centuries before.

> Any account of medieval social and economic thought must also stress the great disdain with which people viewed trade and commerce and the commercial spirit. The medieval way of life was based on custom and tradition; its viability depended on the acceptance by the members of society of that tradition and their place within it. Where the capitalist commercial ethic prevails, greed, selfishness, covetousness, and the desire to better oneself materially or socially are accepted by most people as innate qualities. Yet they were uniformly denounced and reviled in the Middle

Ages. The serfs (and sometimes the lower nobility) tended to be dissatisfied with the traditions and customs of medieval society and thus threatened the stability of the feudal system. It is not surprising, therefore, to find pervasive moral sanctions designed to repress or to mitigate the effects of these motives.[6]

This mind-set, reinforced by the Christian church of that time, was completely altered by the events of following centuries. Wealth accumulation became not only appropriate but laudatory. Trade and commerce became respectable and were seen as beneficial to everyone. Education–or human capital, as economists call it–shifted from teaching how to reproduce the past to teaching that the future must be different and better. The entire worldview changed so that growth and the prospect of plenty replaced the static, no-growth subsistence life of earlier times. The productivity of machinery and ideas brought the prospect of a brighter future and salvation from a life of subsistence. No biblical writers could have discussed the ethical implications of capital productivity with any credibility because it would have been so foreign to their audience.

Some people argue, because of the stories of rapid wealth accumulation and references to interest returns on savings, that biblical writers understood capital productivity. However, wealth accumulations described in the Bible typically came from sporadic increases in natural productivity, not from machine productivity. The seven years of feast and seven years of famine in Egypt during the time of Joseph exemplify how wealth was viewed in biblical times. Land and cattle could bring amazing increases on occasion, but eventual famine and decline were inevitable. Over time, there was no prospect for sustained economic growth for society.

The passages on interest are particularly revealing. The parable of the talents (Matt. 25:14-30) is often used to argue that productive capital was a part of New Testament thinking. A strong case can be made against that view. Interest returns on loans derive from four sources in the modern world: (1) The productivity of capital means that a dollar of consumption foregone today will buy a tool that may return a dollar and a half tomorrow. Part of the fifty-cent increase is shared with the lender as interest. (2) Someone who needs money for present consumption is willing to promise a richer person some interest incentive to lend him money. Wherever present consumption is preferred to future consumption, it bears a cost. Economists call this the time-preference reason for interest. (3) There is always a risk involved in lending money or anything else of value. It might not be returned, or might not be returned in full. The borrower might die, the business enterprise might fail, or any number of other unforeseen problems might make it impossible for the debtor to repay the loan. Lenders try to reduce this risk by charging interest on loans so that loans paid off, including interest, make up for those that are delinquent. (4) In an economy with an expanding money supply, inflation frequently reduces the purchasing power of money. This means that repayment for loans comes in money of lower value than the money initially loaned. Lenders factor their inflation forecasts into their interest rates.

All four of these factors, then, affect interest rates, but any one of them is sufficient incentive to charge interest on a loan. In Bible times it was the time-preference factor that most affected interest rates. Old Testament law, however, argued that this type of interest was not ethical. In the context of the times, it is easy to see why interest was considered wrong. If the loan was used for some needy person's consumption, it should either be given as charity or at least kept on the books as an interest-free loan in hopes of more prosperous times for the debtor. To extract a return from the poor was considered inhumane. Even today, when people give money to poor people who need help for basic living, it is not customary to charge interest. Thus welfare payments by the state require neither interest nor repayment. The interest in the parable of the talents could be seen merely as return on consumption loans rather than as proof of a productive-capital concept in the ancient world. In short, the mention of interest in Scripture is not proof that a concept of production capital existed at that time.

The key idea to keep in mind when reading the biblical passages is that first-century people had no developed understanding of savings as productive capital or tools that could increase production later. Instead, they saw saving as hoarding, which amounted to selfish behavior when others did not have enough for immediate consumption. Had the farmer in Luke 12 set aside some of his output to create better seed or a new tool of production so that he could double his output in the following year, Jesus might have praised him for effective planning toward the goal of solving hunger in society.

In summary, the New Testament writers viewed wealth as basically an accumulation of goods that put more consumption power into the hands of the wealthy few at the expense of the working majority. The accumulations of the rich did not enhance productive capacity in future years or create jobs for anyone. Instead, they fostered greater disparities of lifestyle in society. Wealth was the vehicle to more luxurious living.

From this orientation the New Testament consistently condemns riches and wealth. To become rich was automatically to be more concerned for self than for others, since it meant securing one's own future before caring about current economic suffering. How could such an individual possibly be a participant in the kingdom of God that Jesus was initiating? Only through a miracle of God, if at all (Matt. 19:24, 26; Luke 18:24-25, 27).

Not only did accumulating wealth contradict kingdom principles, but also the preoccupation with wealth was a rich person's constant temptation. "No slave can serve two masters; for a slave will either hate the one and love the other, or be devoted to the one and despise the other. You cannot serve God and wealth" (Luke 16:13). To run an earthly empire while being a disciple in God's kingdom was viewed as a basic contradiction by Jesus and the New Testament writers.

More could be made of this teaching. We might interpret the passages concerned with wealth as showing that preoccupation with wealth is inevitable for the rich unless they give it away in acts of charity. At the very least, the temptations the wealthy face are not easy to overcome, even for the most committed person. Consequently, wealth was condemned in Bible times because it was hoarded and because it posed enormous temptations of idolatry.

It would be inappropriate to downplay the sharp condemnation of wealth in Scripture simply because productive wealth is now more common than hoarded wealth. The danger of idolatry is present in all times. However, it is important to recognize the new category of wealth as one to which Scripture does not speak. In other words, it is inappropriate to condemn wealthy businesspersons today by using the anti-wealth passages of Scripture if their wealth is accumulated in productive tools for socially desirable output and they successfully resist the temptations of being rich. In the next chapter, we will consider how a believer might defend against the dangers of productive wealth. At this point it is only necessary to distinguish between first-century hoarded wealth and modern productive wealth.

Scripture Condemns Hoarding Wealth

Because accumulated wealth in biblical times was hoarded wealth, rather than productive wealth, it is criticized frequently in Scripture. However, some argue that wealth is not always rebuked in Scripture. Jacob's accumulation and Job's faithfulness amid enormous riches are not subjects for anti-wealth teaching, but neither are they affirmations of wealth, any more than Jacob's deceitfulness in acquiring the birthright is appropriate behavior for gaining a desired end. The Old Testament stories weave together events and teaching in ways that can be sorted out only by an appeal to the prominent themes of Scripture that occur throughout the entire text. Concern for lavish wealth is one of those themes because there was a perception that one person's

wealth was detrimental to the masses, not beneficial. Passages
that indicate otherwise are usually historical narratives rather than
normative teaching. A chart showing the differences in income
use by the ancient and modern worlds appears in figure 5.1. The
significant difference between the two orientations is that productive investment appears in the center column but not in the left
column. Discerning the meaning of that difference is an important
part of the next chapter, but this chapter has presented the view
that productive wealth may be appropriate to hold since it generates increasing future production for society to consume.

Figure 5.1

Biblical Approaches to Ancient and Modern Uses of Wealth

Ancient	Modern	Biblical Approach
Consumption	Consumption	Modest living taught in Scripture
Charity	Charity	Required of believers
Hoarded future consumption	Hoarded future consumption	Condemned by Scripture
	Productive capital	Not treated specifically in Scripture

To summarize, because the biblical writers did not live in a
world that emphasized capital tools of production, and because
their world was basically a no-growth, steady-state environment,
Scripture does not offer a perspective on accumulated wealth in
the form of capital goods. This perspective is left for believers to
develop as the world continues to move into a capital-oriented
economy. Sadly, believers have not pursued this task carefully, so
businesspeople today are criticized by many believers who use
Scripture as if they lived in a first-century world. Also, the businessperson and those sympathetic to the business community frequently see no alternative but to seek scriptural texts, usually in

the wisdom literature of the Old Testament, as counter-evidence that the anti-wealth tone in Scripture is really not there. Neither of these improper approaches has been helpful to the community of faith.

The next chapter will attempt to describe how believers should relate to one another on economic matters in a way that will be biblically sound and yet take into account the different economic world in which we live. The dangers of accumulated wealth are still quite real, and believers today must not take them lightly–even if the accumulation is in productive wealth.

Discussion Questions

1. This chapter argues that wealth in the form of productive investment is not condemned in Scripture because it did not exist then as it does today. Can you think of any Bible passages that might relate to productive investment as we perceive it?

2. If our economy today were a constant-sum environment as the biblical people understood their world to be, would we have different views on economic justice? If so, how might our thinking about economic distribution change?

3. Would the purchasing and storing of gold bars, non-sentimental antiques, or baseball cards be present-day examples of hoarding? *No*

    These are pure examples of
    time & auction based values.
    All of these items had to be 'purchased',
    producing re distribution of value / currency.
    All have intrinsic value (including sold).
    'intangible'

6

A Radical Economic Model for Today

B y now it should be clear that the complicated, machine-oriented economy in which we live has made the task of interpreting Scripture more difficult. The categories of income use listed in the last chapter provide an agenda for discussion. In the ancient world, consumption, charity, and hoarding were the categories deemed relevant. Hoarding was considered sinful because in a constant-sum economy that was at or near subsistence, any hoarding was viewed as taking from others what they needed at the moment for survival.

The New and Old Testament critique of riches is not focused on the earning of income but on its misuse. The misuse could be in the form of either hoarding or consumption. A typical charge to the high-income earner is found in 1 Timothy 6:17-19:

> As for those who in the present age are rich, command them not to be haughty, or to set their hopes on the uncertainty of riches, but rather on God who richly provides us with everything for our enjoyment. They are to do good, to be rich in good works, generous, and ready to share, thus storing up for themselves the treasure of a good foundation for the future, so that they may take hold of the life that really is life.

Some have used this passage to justify high consumption because God "provides us with everything for our enjoyment." We can see the fallacy of this interpretation by beginning at verse 3 rather than at verse 17. In these verses Timothy critiques contentious people "who are depraved in mind and bereft of the truth, imagining that godliness is a means of gain. Of course, there is a great gain in godliness combined with contentment; for we brought nothing into the world, so that we can take nothing out of it; but if we have food and clothing, we will be content with these" (1 Tim. 6:5-8). If consumption was to be modest and hoarding was wrong, then that left only charity as an outlet for high earnings. Tithing is mentioned in the New Testament but not highlighted. The expectation was that, after a modest living was secured, the rest was to be used to promote justice, mercy, and faith (Matt. 23:23). The Old Testament notion of offerings above a tithe amounts to a similar teaching.

The term *contentment* was used in the Greek philosophical sense to mean an ideal situation where no aid or support is needed. In 2 Corinthians 9:8, the only other place it is used in the New Testament, contentment relates to the necessities of life. This passage is not an attack on rich people, but it is a statement that God values modest living.

Another example of this concern is found in Luke 16:19-31. Here Jesus tells of the nameless rich man who lived in luxury while Lazarus, a beggar, lay at his gate. The implication is strong that the rich man's unwillingness to redistribute some of his income to Lazarus was a factor in his damnation. This theme is consistent with Jesus' commentary on the rich young ruler in Matthew 19:24 and with other teachings, including the behavior of the early church recorded in the book of Acts.

Indeed, in a context devoid of productive capital, the biblical teaching makes logical sense. The prophets' vicious criticism of accumulated wealth (see the book of Amos) and the stinging charges against riches in the New Testament are not overstatements or utopian, egalitarian dreaming. Instead, they were legitimate demands from a God who cared about income distribution enough to challenge the rich to live modestly and give mightily. The criticism is not against the high income that some apparently had, but rather against how much they consumed and how little they gave away.

When one moves to the modern world, things become more complicated because of the additional category to which income can be allocated. Productive investment now becomes another way to use income. As discussed before, this area is not mentioned in Scripture; neither was it a prominent concern in the history of the church until relatively recently, when machines became important in the production process. Thus believers must use careful discernment to allocate their income effectively. The task is more difficult than it was in the first century because now there are three legitimate uses for money: hoarding, or nonproductive investment as it might be called, is still as wrong as it was in the ancient world; that leaves consumption, charity, and productive investment.

The fact that the church has said little about how believers should handle financial matters is a tragedy that needs correcting. Typically the only principle articulated is that believers should give at least 10 percent of their income to charity, but beyond that believers are on their own. Investment and consumption are matters for private consideration. Market price signals and individual preferences alone guide decision making. Believers as a group usually do not become involved in the moral dilemmas of these choices. In fact, financial secrecy is thought to be a virtue. Presumably, too much information only creates gossip, jealousy, and dissension. This is evidence of how the church has accepted secular values in economic matters.

Striving for Responsibility

What follows is a discussion of how believers might become more responsible in the categories of income generation, consumption, charity, and productive investment. In other words, what should the relationships labeled *A* in chapter 4 look like in a church that wants to be faithful, both individually and collectively, in economic matters?

Choices in Income Generation

Believers are employed in a wide variety of secular and Christian organizations. One might judge their usefulness to society by the salary level they can command. Generally, the higher their pay, the more valuable their contribution; but it is clear that the value of the contribution is measured by secular standards. For example, a brewmaster might make more money than a nurse, but a believer will consider other matters before becoming a brewmaster. Nearly every Christian job-seeker needs wider input than just salary figures. This is where the community of believers can help in discerning a person's gifts and evaluating the moral issues that surround a particular job offer. When I came out of graduate school, the body of believers in my church convinced me that I could serve God better in a job that offered little more than half of what the highest-alternative position offered. I knew they were right, but without them I probably would have made a different choice.

Questions of gift discernment among believers must be generalized beyond simply staffing Sunday school and church outreach programs. When a community of believers gives its blessing to a member's job, additional involvement in economic issues becomes less difficult. It must be emphasized that the size of one's income is neither the key concern nor a measure of one's worth or influence in the church. Some may earn high pay and receive the blessing of the believers, who recognize the reward that a market brings to highly skilled people. Others may value leisure more and willingly make the trade-offs required to follow their preferences. The ramifications of this option should be discussed in community as well. In short, the community of faith must be more involved in work and leisure choices and in the concerns that come to people as they live out their choices.

Choices in Consumption

The first claim on family income is usually consumption. People generally determine the standard of living that they will maintain and then protect it as carefully as possible. One component of the standard of living is the growth rate people seek in their lifestyle. How are the consumption standards set? What values influence those standards and the plans for future consumption? The answers to these questions are fairly easy to find in the secular world. In general, income levels determine consumption standards, and the hope is for as rapid growth as possible. Perpetual growth is a dominant Western value.

There is little evidence that Christians follow a different pattern, except for those who choose simple living and low pay in order to enter special areas of Christian service. Perhaps the area of consumption is the most serious blind spot contemporary Christians have in the exercise of their faith. There are several reasons for this. First, any dollar spent on consumption is unavailable for charity or productive investment. Second, people are less inclined to relate to those who have living standards appreciably above their own. Thus, those with substantially above-average lifestyles limit the range of their ministry. Third, an abundance of things can easily create a feeling of self-sufficiency that tends to crowd out God. Scripture abounds with statements on the risks of high living. Fourth, an abundance of things predisposes one to protect those things in ways that require more expenditures on insurance and crime deterrence. Fifth, luxurious living makes it hard to identify with poor people everywhere.

In view of all this, why is the church so silent on consumption? The answer is complex, but certainly part of the problem is the ambiguities of determining what is luxury, what is need, and when *things* are becoming too important. The common phrase, "Everything is relative," can sidetrack any preacher brave enough to suggest restraint of lifestyle. In fact, everything *is* relative in these matters, and that is the most compelling reason why the community of believers must use its God-given gifts of discernment to enable the Christian to make responsible use of resources. Some suggestions may be helpful, although for many these suggestions will seem more like meddling than preaching.

First, the amount that a typical family spends on itself should be within some carefully conceived range around the average of the community in which it is called to minister. For example, if the average family consumption in the community around a church is $30,000, then members might try to have consumption patterns within a range of $20,000 to $40,000. This is not an effort to introduce a legalistic rule but to establish an expectation from which believers deviate only with careful thought, prayer, and the blessing of their community of faith. Some may have good reasons for living above or below this expectation; the community of faith should affirm more extreme lifestyles for those with special circumstances.

Thus believers can ensure that deviations do not occur automatically, out of habit, or because of rapid income changes, but after consideration of issues related to the church's ministry and a particular family's needs. Christian groups often have discovered a new dimension of faith and found the exercise of stewardship easier and more rewarding when members are willing to share and be accountable to each other.

This suggestion appears less radical than at first blush when we realize that living standards are usually set not in a vacuum but relative to some social group. Therefore, it seems important to make the values of the church the reference point for Christians rather than the values of a secular group. Secular norms invariably point to continually higher living standards as evidence of success and importance. If the church articulates no values, then the standards of the world will become the norm for the believer. I sometimes try to raise the consciousness of my students with stories of high consumption behavior. I ask the students whether the case presented offends their moral sensitivities. Some invariably insist that, no matter how outrageous the example may seem, no one has the right to pass judgement on another's decision. As an experiment, list some cases that would morally offend you. Try to develop a continuum of moral sensitivity relating to major purchases, and then watch what happens to it as you get older.

One complication of establishing consumption norms like those suggested is that those who fall below the consumption range will need a subsidy from the church. Usually this is done only for those in mission work or church employment, or in cases of accident or disaster. In these situations, the church evaluates each case on its merits and offers help where it seems appropriate. There is no reason why poorer families in the church should not apply for help in the same manner to have their consumption level brought up to the minimum standard considered appropriate by the community of faith. Although this seems too radical for many, it is far less radical than the communal treasury practice of many intentional communities across the United States and around the world.

Choices in Giving

The next category of income allocation is charity. Since the church has typically preached a 10 percent tithing rule as a minimum for believers, there is less that needs to be said here except to notice that in our modern environment, reduced consumption by the wealthy may not necessarily end up in charity. It may also be directed toward productive investment, which is a legitimate use of income.

One facet of giving, too often overlooked, is the joy that generous sharing brings to the believer. The real blessings of giving are intangible rather than material, although we frequently talk of God's blessings in material terms. Nowhere in the Bible is a lavish standard of living promised to those who share their resources with others. The much-abused passage in Matthew 6:33 is perhaps the strongest directive to believers to practice a more explicit economic model of sharing than they presently do. The command to "strive first for the kingdom of God and his righteousness" requires adopting the characteristics described earlier in chapter 4, and the things that will be given are the basic needs of life. From Matthew 6:31 it is obvious that these are food, clothing, and shelter. Although our list may be a bit longer, it is easy to see that luxurious consumption is the antithesis of all that this section of the Sermon on the Mount is about.

If material sufficiency, not plenty, is a reward for giving, and if believers already have their basic needs met, is there a blessing in giving? Certainly! The joy of helping in the cause of the church may be the greatest undertapped renewable resource the world will ever have. That joy is multiplied because giving draws one closer to the programs of the church and its caring, discerning process. Being closer to the church affects one's witness in many ways including, most importantly, how one's children view faith and practice. When the church becomes the focus of one's life, the model being developed here becomes possible, and the world can see an exciting way of life that makes concrete what the call to faith is all about. In short, giving puts one's treasure and one's heart in the church.

Because the most obvious expression of the church is the local congregation, it is important to give the majority of one's contribution to the local church rather than to organizations that have far less accountability to their supporters. One whose heart is in the church views the joy and blessings spoken of in Scripture differently from one whose treasure is in the world of material gain and high consumption.

The Problem of Hoarding

Hoarding is difficult to define in modern society. Because of extremely sophisticated and efficient financial markets and fractional reserve banking, most savings are quickly funneled into economic activity. Many will argue that, short of burying valuables in the ground, it is impossible to hoard in a society of efficient markets. Certainly it is true that markets make nearly everything interchangeable so that a dollar saved somewhere becomes a productive investment elsewhere.

In addition, the idea that services are as important to economic well-being as are goods means that many things that persons might do with their income are productive. A valuable painting gives people pleasure as truly as a loom makes clothing for them. Speculating in a market performs the valuable service of spreading risk that others prefer to avoid. Even burying money in the backyard has few ill effects on the economy because the Federal Reserve Board expands the money supply if a shortage of loanable funds occurs. Thus money is available for productive uses anyway.

Many are concerned that they are hoarding when they build up a retirement fund for their future. This is a particularly difficult issue because of the way provision for the elderly has changed over the years. With the dispersion of the family, the elderly are left to provide for themselves. In place of a family farm, which in many cases had value greater than many retirement accounts, there are retirement centers that are costly. Not to provide for life after work is to assume that the government will provide for retirement needs. Because so many people now outlive their abilty to work the task of lifetime financial planning is essential. Believers should have lifetime financial plans that begin early in life and include complete estate planning. If this is done wisely, the individual will have an adequate retirement and the church will have more funds sooner for its ministries. Again, because of efficient financial markets, this concern about retirement investments relates more to the issue of lifetime consumption planning than it does to the problem of hoarding. Excessive retirement fund accumulations due to an obsession with future security are harmful for reasons other than hoarding.[1]

In short, the concept of hoarding in modern times is relevant, but observing hoarding in practice is virtually impossible. Most likely the relevant framework is one that simply examines investment along a continuum from least productive to most productive rather than comparing productive with nonproductive uses of wealth. To some degree this continuum is part of the discussion of investment that we will take up shortly.

Before examining productive investment as a category of income use, we should observe that the effects of hoarding in today's market-oriented economies are not as damaging as the effects of hoarding would have been on a more primitive economy. Today's flexible money supply and efficient capital markets offset hoarding's normally contractionary effects on the larger economy. In other words, the very things that make hoarding hard to define also diminish its negative effect on the economy.

On the other hand, the effect that an accumulation of claims on future income has on one's approach to the Christian life can hardly be overemphasized, whether or not the claims come from productive or nonproductive investment. Both temptations and opportunities for service grow for people with potential for great accumulation. The temptations come in the areas of self-sufficiency, pride, mistrust of the poor, use of power and influence, and the shortage of time available for the pursuit of faith and church life. The opportunities come in some areas of witness, the ability to contribute more to charity, increased organizational and managerial expertise, and the socially desirable output that results if the accumulation is productive. It is a thesis of this book that God never intended people to balance these temptations and opportunities without the help of a caring community of faith. This concept will be pursued later in the chapter.

Choices in Productive Investment

The last category of income use is productive investment. We argued earlier that Scripture gives little direction on this topic, so those who seek to apply the principles of the kingdom of God to their investment behavior must do some careful thinking.

Productive investment can be defined as expenditures that buy tools to produce goods and services in the future. A tractor, drill press, or factory building will require resources that would otherwise be available for consumption. A dollar spent on a drill press cannot go to feed someone starving today. However, if the drill press is purchased today, the output of the factory may be enough to save more than one person next year. In other words, the businessperson may be caught in the ethical dilemma of saving one person now or two later. The technological age of our place in history has brought on these time-related kinds of ethical dilemmas.

Businesspersons now have three legitimate outlets for their income. After the consumption level is determined and the charity minimum is given, their remaining income can go toward productive capital investment or additional charity. How this division of surplus is determined is partly a business decision and partly a decision for which believers need guidance from the community of faith. At least, they should be able to articulate how the mission of the church and the mission of the business enterprise are complementary and how each will be served by the available funds. When proprietors choose to expand the business and give less to the church, they may be making a wise and responsible decision. At the same time, their primary group of believers should be available as a sounding board to check the rationale that led to the decision.

It is unfair for believers to criticize businesspersons who are wealthy because of extensive assets in productive machinery. It is also inappropriate for businesspeople to build productive empires without any counsel from a community of faith that can help guard against temptations inherent in the competitive, self-serving economic world. Indeed, Christian businesspersons need the church to help discern right from wrong and good from best in certain business decisions, just as much as the church needs businesspeople for their expertise and contributions.

The term *businessperson* is understood in too narrow a fashion most of the time. Participants in the work force invest productively when they take time for job training. One of the most widely accepted forms of investment in modern times is the human capital built up in education. Formal education and job training of all kinds are investment activities that nearly everyone engages in at some time, and they represent business decisions that the community of faith should not take lightly. Some churches commission their young people in a special service as they enter new stages of their education, particularly college. This blessing given to an investment by young people should also accompany significant investments by people in other areas of life so that they, too, can proceed with the confidence that their efforts are important to the life of the church, or can alter their plans if sufficient doubts have been raised about the wisdom of a decision.

Involving the Church

This interaction among believers on matters that concern activity in everyday life increases the quality of church life and helps in the believer's effort to meet the temptations and opportunities of the modern economy. It also becomes a powerful witness to a world that finds the individual pursuit of happiness shallow and unfulfilling.

Given the present state of many churches and the prevailing view that one's financial business is a private affair, some may find it hard to imagine how mutual accountability in finances can become part of the Christian agenda. Yet, the more closely a body of believers models the teaching of 1 Corinthians 12 and 13, the more feasible the prospect of mutual accountability in financial matters becomes.

What are some of the advantages and disadvantages of this model for believers today? What are some examples of how the model might work in practice? Here is a list of *advantages* of this model, followed by more elaboration:

1. Key decisions on difficult issues of lifestyle are worked out in community rather than by the prevailing social trend or the individual alone. Individual autonomy in personal consumption and business practice is, to some degree, sacrificed.

2. Large disparities in living standards among believers are carefully examined.
3. Believers can live in the confidence that they have the blessing of the church on their lifestyle.
4. God, through his church, is in control of 100 percent of the resources of his people, not just 10 percent.
5. Society at large, by seeing the Christians, will understand more readily that there is more to life than material things.
6. Questions regarding the appropriateness of various investments and jobs are dealt with collectively so that individual vested interests take second place to an unbiased search for the will of God in the investment decision.
7. The model encourages deeper involvement in the life of the fellowship.

For those who believe that the secular models of resource allocation are appropriate for the church, these advantages may seem like disadvantages. Many people desire individual autonomy in economic matters without accountability to other believers. Some argue that satisfactory guidelines for the Christian in economic matters are generated by the rules of the market. This chapter argues that such standards are not sufficient.

The Church: Basic Unit of Economic Decision making

The approach presented here questions such individualism because of a fundamental assumption that the basic unit for Christian action is the church, not the individual. That assumption must be substantiated if the preceding model is to appear credible.

To say that the community of faith is the basic unit for Christian action means that the church gives its blessing to the behavior of its members in specific ways. It also means that behavior inconsistent with the expectations of the fellowship of believers is not overlooked, but dealt with according to biblical principles of discipline, particularly those spelled out in 2 Timothy 2:23-26.

The need for a committed community of faith as a primary unit for action is evident from passages like Ephesians 4:11-12, where the diversity of gifts is discussed: "The gifts he gave were that some would be apostles, some prophets, some evangelists, some pastors and teachers, to equip the saints for the work of ministry, for building up the body of Christ...." Clearly, spiritual wisdom is not complete in any individual, so making important decisions alone means shortchanging the effectiveness of the church. To paraphrase the passage in Ephesians, one might say that if the church does not incorporate its gifts into decision processes about lifestyle and business practice, it will detract from the perfecting of the saints, the work of the ministry, and the edification of the church in those areas of life.

The passages that compare the community of faith to a body (1 Cor. 12:12-31) and a temple "built together spiritually" (Eph. 2:20-22) are beautiful illustrations of the interaction in community that is necessary to provide a "dwelling place for God" (Eph. 2:22). One chapter later, in Ephesians 3:10, Paul declares that it is through the church that God's plan for creation is made apparent, "so that through the church the wisdom of God in its rich variety might now be made known to the rulers and authorities in the heavenly places." In 2 Timothy 2:22 Paul admonished Timothy to avoid evil by immersing himself in the fellowship of Christians: "Shun youthful passions and pursue righteousness, faith, love and peace, *along with* [emphasis added] those who call on the Lord from a pure heart." What is clear is that the community of faith is to be far more in the life of believers than an organizational structure for group education, corporate worship, and large helping projects.

What is surprising is that the church in twentieth-century America has been able to read the Bible and ignore so many dimensions of commitment. Many churches practice little careful discernment. Positive discipline and group norm setting are rarely experienced. Too often, individual effort is expended to appropriate the Holy Spirit without the guidance of a committed group of believers, despite the teaching in Ephesians 2:22 and elsewhere. Frequently, institutional structure encumbers the breakthrough of kingdom qualities. The key ingredient required to reverse this situation is found in 1 Corinthians 13, where lists of religious acts are presented as worthless apart from abiding *agape* love. This love provides content and quality to the commitment needed in the church. Without it, all hope for a dynamic community of faith is lost. The less the people of God appropriate this caring love among themselves, the more unrealistic, idealistic, and improbable the church as a true community of faith will seem.

Criticism is easy, but constructive building is difficult. Some find consolation in the fact that, in the latter part of 1 Corinthians 13, Paul recognizes that perfection will not occur, weaknesses will be present, love will seem far away, and we must wait until the close of history to understand love completely. However, the directive in the first verse of the next chapter is to pursue the way of love eagerly and diligently. That leaves the church with no choice but to build its behavioral models, assuming that believers should strive for a more complete, committed fellowship of love. From a Christian point of view, models based on individual autonomy are simply inadequate.

The *second advantage* of the model deals with the large disparities in lifestyle that exist among Christians of the same church. Where these disparities exist through circumstance and not by choice, little effective interaction can occur. One economist, in discussing the need to have communities of faith disciple each other on matters of consumption, writes, "We will not be successful in becoming an effective 'consumption watchers' group for each other unless we deal with the differences in income levels among us. I cannot help you to deal with your desires if my income is higher than yours and if I insist it is my income alone, to spend as I choose."[2] In the context in which it is written, it is clear that this reference to income corresponds to the consumption part of the model developed here.

To see more clearly why consumption differences create barriers to communication, visualize a hypothetical lawyer who spends $60,000 a year on his family, telling a hypothetical elementary school teacher, who spends $25,000 a year on his family, not to eat out in a restaurant, to forego a vacation, to get a babysitter and have his wife work, or to abandon family plans for a third child. Since the lawyer has made no similar adjustments, the interchange that follows could sound like this:

Teacher: It doesn't seem fair that I must make these adjustments when you can live as you please.

Lawyer: Why not? I earn my income, so there is no reason why I can't spend it.

Teacher: But I work as long and as hard as you do, and my job helps society as much as yours.

Lawyer: If that were true, your pay would equal mine.

From here the discussion degenerates quickly.

Teacher: Not so. Your pay is higher because the legal profession has created a monopoly for itself in order to charge unrealistically high rates. The legal profession even resisted the law allowing their members to advertise charges.

Lawyer: Not so. Nothing stopped you from entering law school and competing with me. These issues are really a matter of choice.

Teacher: ....

These discussions rarely, if ever, occur among church members because of the dissension and hard feelings that would result. But how many times have exchanges similar to this one occurred in people's minds, and what has been the effect of these thoughts on the life of the fellowship? To prevent these thoughts, church people have hidden their financial affairs from view as much as possible. The lawyer wants to be appreciated, so he will try not to flaunt his income; the teacher wants respect, so he will hide his financial struggles. Both need each other in the church. One has teaching skills, and the other can help meet the budget and give counsel to the church. But the atmosphere of love and sharing and trust does not exist.[3]

Some suggest that low-income persons truly committed to Christ will not be affected by income disparities in the church, so that this conversation is unrealistic. This is true if the church has implicitly or explicitly defined an appropriate consumption range that includes both the teacher and the lawyer. However, if no such range is defined, each individual will define for oneself what a Christian lifestyle should be. The resulting confusion detracts from congregational unity, hindering the mission of the church. The least the church must do is to help the person in need. But if there is no understanding of the definition of need, how can it do this?

A wealthy person buys an air conditioner, a dishwasher, a set of golf clubs, or a van to meet a "need." Yet a poor person who comes to the church for help, expressing those same needs, probably will not be accommodated. The church is forced into the position of saying that the rich and the poor, in many areas of life, do not have the same needs, or that the rich should be allowed to consume above their needs in areas of luxury. Hiding this dilemma with the hope that strong commitment on the part of the poor will make the problem disappear means exposing oneself to severe temptation.

What are people really saying when they declare publicly or by action that they have the right to live at a standard much above that of the other members in the church? They are suggesting, first, that they deserve more because of their skills, ability, or value to society; and second, that they were fortunate enough to be at the right place at the right time. In other words, they were smart, hardworking, lucky, or all three. Yet a good mind and good fortune are gifts from God to his church, not to individuals alone, and a person's contribution to production is a response to God for those gifts. How many times have we heard individuals testify how the Lord has blessed them? Yet from 1 Corinthians 12 it is clear that the blessing was meant to be shared in love for the benefit of the church. "Now there are varieties of gifts, but the same Spirit; and there are varieties of service, but the same Lord; and there are varieties of activities, but it is the same God who activates all of them in everyone. To each is given the manifestation of the Spirit for the common good" (12:4-7).

Later in this passage, Paul indicates that those with less glamorous skills are blessed no less by God, even though their monetary income may not be great. To be intelligent and lucky, from God's point of view, entitles one to no more or less consumption because of those blessings, even if it does bring a person high income. High earnings come to those with productive gifts, and they should not reduce their work effort simply because their consumption may not rise with their income.

If these views are present in the church, believers will desire to find ways to close the large lifestyle gaps in the church. The model presented here can help in this effort.

The Blessing of the Church

The *third advantage* of this model is that, if they apply it, believers will have the blessing of the church on their lifestyle. This will minimize the suspicions and mistrust that can otherwise occur, as well as the guilt that some feel because of uncertainty regarding their standard of living. It will never remove the tension of consuming in a world of scarcity, but the tension is shared by the community of faith and provides a constant reminder to that community that all lifestyle norms need review from time to time. Such a review will ensure that the *fourth advantage* of the model is achieved: that all resource use, not just 10 percent, will be considered as part of the witness of faith and subject to the blessing of the community of faith.

Being Salt and Light

The *fifth advantage*, providing a witness to the larger society, fits into the church's function as salt and light to the world (Matt. 5:13-16). It is not necessary to document the despair of many in the secular kingdom, both rich and poor, who have made the struggle for increased living standards a religion as they serve wealth as their god (Matt. 6:24, 32; Col. 3:5). This is one way the church can show that it has a better, more meaningful way of meeting the material needs of people.

Current attempts at mutual sharing through church-sponsored insurance programs have successfully re-integrated into the church some functions that the church earlier abandoned. For example, the Mennonite denomination has its own investment fund, a congregational college tuition-sharing program, auto and health insurance programs, retirement centers, disaster service organizations, and many local sharing services.

Years ago I was a member of a denominational regional auto insurance plan. There had been a rather heavy claim one year, so the pool of funds for claims had fallen below the desirable level. Instead of raising the premiums, the company sent a letter to all members explaining the problem and asking for donations according to the members' ability to pay. Gifts from members eliminated the problem. Another feature of that insurance arrangement was that every six months a list of names with claims paid was sent to all members. There was some incentive to avoid claims since no one wanted to be an obvious drain on the fund.

Many denominations have similar programs, and others are forming. There is no reason why this experience shouldn't encourage the church to support more localized efforts that may illustrate to society that Christianity does make a difference at the financial level. The church at large should be building evidence that Christianity has a significant economic impact on the lives of those who profess it.

Finally, we cannot lose sight of the fact that the world is watching to see if believers live out their faith. Do we contribute to larger income disparities in society, or do we lean against the tendency for severe income inequalities to exist. One day on the streets of Moscow, a large late-model Mercedes was stalled with its hood raised. As the citizens passed by, I observed the satisfaction that many received from seeing an apparently wealthy man stranded in the heat of the day. Having such an expensive car when so many were struggling for food seemed wrong to the Russians. I suggest that the same kind of feeling is universal and is even more offensive if the person displaying wealth is a Christian. Let us not destroy our witness by high consumption and then compound the problem by acting as if those offended are jealous or mean-spirited. There is ample evidence that Jesus and the prophets were concerned about high consumption, not only compared with believers within the church, but compared with society at large.

Giving Guidance

The *sixth advantage* of the model relates to the direction that the model, functioning effectively, gives to those who are asking serious questions about their financial involvement in secular society. For example, relevant questions might be:

1. Should I invest money in the stock of a company that produces weapons or tobacco or even luxury items that have little, if any, functional use?
2. Does the college I support have its endowment invested in socially responsible companies?
3. Are the business practices of the companies I invest in just and fair to the consumer, and does that matter?
4. Should I work where I must join and support a militant union that demands pay hikes far above productivity growth?
5. As an employee, what responsibility do I have in a firm whose business ethics are unchristian (e.g., discrimination or payoffs)?

All of these questions and more are difficult to answer with an across-the-board response. Each is a special case and demands the attention of a fellowship that can approach the situation with less bias than can any one person. When the majority feeling of the group grows into consensus, the decision is made, and the binding and loosing process can occur. This process cannot be taken lightly. For example, in Wisconsin, seven Catholic religious communities have formed an organization to research investment sources, looking for those that benefit society from a Christian point of view. At least one mutual fund investment company serves those who seek investments in industries where no war-related products are produced, fair employment practices are followed, and international development is fostered.[4] Many other funds have special moral criteria for investing as well, and new ones could be formed. When believers become serious about moral dimensions of economic behavior, many creative expressions of faith can develop.

Gaining Strength from the Group

The *last* listed *advantage* of the model, that of deeper involvement in the fellowship of the church, involves a principle of human nature well known to the Christian and the non-Christian. When difficult tasks lie ahead, group support and specific measures of progress are invaluable in bringing results.

For example, most people recognize that physical exercise is necessary for good health. Yet it is a rare individual who continues an exercise program faithfully alone. Successful joggers jog with others. The discipline of the friend helps to overcome the monotony and drudgery of the task. Also, specific measures reveal when the goal is reached. Jogging became more meaningful to many when they realized that two miles run in under fifteen minutes three times a week could provide enough exercise for good health. Without a defined goal and a support group, difficult tasks become impossible. The same is true in Weight Watchers,

Alcoholics Anonymous, preparing for childbirth, or any other difficult task. The Christian life requires the same dedication.

One of the tasks that requires hard work and discipline is responsible resource use. How unfortunate that few Christians work hard to establish lifestyle norms and support each other by consistently living them! It is meaningful and enjoyable to find ways to conserve; having less must become more satisfying than having more. By developing a spirit of unity in action, Christians can grow into a deeper involvement in faith with each other.

Objections to the Model

Before leaving the discussion of the formal model, we need to look at some of the criticisms or concerns that many have about its operation.

1. High-income earners may have less incentive to earn income if it is not for themselves, and so their productivity may drop.
2. Some may prefer a church grant rather than to work.
3. The group discernment process involves people in decisions in areas where they have no expertise or training.
4. How can one ensure that the group is not simply a collection of friends that gives its blessing to any whimsical request? In other words, what keeps the group balanced?

All of these questions are legitimate and must be taken seriously. The first and second concerns have similar answers: they involve people whose commitment to the fellowship and its purpose is weak. Where Christians amass wealth to live in luxury rather than for the service they can perform with it, they are out of step with the spirit of Scripture and would benefit from a careful study of biblical teaching. If their wealth is not viewed as a tool for service to God and the church, it is unlikely that they will be attracted to a community of faith in the first place—particularly if the teaching of the church is clear and the discipling task of believers is being practiced. Furthermore, a believer is productive in response to God's sufficiency and grace. If less is retained personally and more is given away, the incentive for the Christian to work should not diminish. In fact, when a life of giving is practiced, the joy that results is usually incentive to do more rather than less.

The rich young man of Matthew 19:16-22 wanted to become part of the kingdom of God. But when he realized that his wealth had to be brought under submission, he rejected the kingdom voluntarily. It is interesting that Christ was not inclined to back away from his high demands in order to keep from alienating the rich man, who was probably a faithful tither. Likewise, the church should be clear about its expectations in the area of resource use.

The situation may differ for the person who sees the church as an escape from work. There are those who will apply for consumption grants continuously, seeking a free ride while they contribute little. To counter this, each grant request must be accompanied by full supporting data documenting the reason for the need. Some in the church may be commissioned to involve themselves in worthwhile tasks that do not pay wages or, at best, pay inadequate wages. These would receive grants in the same way missionaries and volunteer workers presently do. In those cases Christians are not offended by those who attempt to raise their own support for service activity.

In other cases, emergencies may arise requiring financial help to fill the gap between needs and income. In still other cases, there may be those who legitimately cannot find work or have handicaps that keep earnings below the acceptable level. In all cases, no one should receive grants without careful review.

The discipling process in these matters involves balancing several principles taught in Scripture. On the one side are the admonitions to carry our own loads, work if we are to eat, and not lack in zeal (Gal. 6:5; 2 Thess. 3:10; Rom. 12:11). On the other side is the command to help a brother or sister in need and to bear one another's burdens (Gal. 6:2; Rom. 12:13; 1 John 3:17). There is no indication that these could not include financial burdens, even though the context of some of the passages refers to moral faults. Decisions on consumption grants will not be easy, especially when admonition is required. But if taken seriously, the process can reward everyone involved.

Nevertheless, the model we are examining should make the process work better because it defines need by the lower level of the consumption range instead of not defining it at all. At present, the church has the same directives regarding the poor that this model suggests, but it has an unstructured way of approaching the problem. Thus it never articulates clearly who really needs help and who needs appropriate encouragement to be productive.

The third objection to the model concerns the decision process. The dynamics of any group are such that those with expertise in a particular area are looked to for leadership in that area. Certainly those within a group who know little about business will not have a strong influence on whether the fellowship affirms a businessperson's plans for investment. The important point is that people in business must describe their intentions, goals, and proposals so that less knowledgeable people can give their support on the grounds of what they can understand and of their trust in the persons involved. This process will help the businesspeople plan with a clear focus on the kingdom goals to which they have committed themselves as members of the church.

One other concern about the decision process is the *decision rule* that is followed. Perhaps the best statement of the decision rule is one of majority rule in the framework of consensus. Many have a political orientation toward decision making and have never shared in a fellowship based on Christian love. Such people will have a difficult time interpreting a process so ambiguous. Where agreement by acclamation isn't possible, the issue is debated, researched, and prayed about. Votes are taken, and the will of the majority is then supported by all those in the fellowship in a manner similar to the current process of choosing congregational officers. The greater the sharing of Christian love in the fellowship, the greater will be the appropriation of the Holy Spirit and the more satisfactory the discerning process.

The last criticism deals with the moorings of the group itself. What keeps it from serving its own interests rather than the purposes of God? True, some fellowships have departed from a serious effort to become the people of God. They reinforce each other's biases and accomplish little. However, it is far easier for individuals to deviate from a commitment on their own than for groups to deviate from the same commitment. What keeps Weight Watchers from encouraging obesity, or Alcoholics Anonymous from throwing huge drinking parties? The answer lies in each group's avowed purpose and commitment to a goal. Alone, it is easy to falter in commitment. The group acts as a balance wheel, constantly calling back into the fold those tempted to stray.

The community of believers is that balance wheel for the Christian. If the group is serious about its faith and uses Scripture as its anchor, it has a far better chance of serving the kingdom of God effectively than do individuals apart from a group. When a fellowship loses its moorings and no persuasive voice within it calls for renewal, the kingdom of God ceases to be served in that gathering. However, this is unlikely to occur until long after the individuals, on their own, have departed from the faith.

Is This Model Too Idealistic to Be Useful?

Some say an emphatic yes to this question. They contend that as long as we live in a world of selfishness and are imperfect Christians, this model is doomed to fail. Some would simply call it impractical rather than idealistic. There is no doubt that it would be difficult for believers to attain in modern Western culture. It would be far easier to avoid the economic issues and assume that God is not concerned with our behavior in that area. But Scripture simply does not give us that option.

One observation that seems pertinent is that the church tends toward this kind of model whenever it is persecuted or is disenfranchised within a society. From the early church on, persecution led to tight communities of faith with mutual aid and caring. During the Reformation, the Anabaptists related to each other in ways similar to that described here. Sometimes there was a more mandatory tone to the practices than I have suggested here. Today the need for renewed community is much more disguised. The culture is not openly hostile to believers who do not challenge its structures. We are not forced to take a stand that is costly. Nevertheless, as I will discuss in chapter 13, the temptation to sell out to the spirit of the age has never been stronger than it is today. The wolf is in sheep's clothing in our time, and we need to work harder to make the biblical ideals operational.

Discussion Questions

1. In what sense is the model developed here radical?
2. For many, this chapter goes from preaching to meddling. Do you agree or disagree? How can you tell the difference?
3. The issues of productive and nonproductive investment have been debated in some form or another for many years. Would you put different values on the acquisition of gold or nonsentimental antiques than you would on a farm implement if each of these expenditures brought the same return on your money?
4. Did you arrive at your standard of living by a careful and prayerful consideration of what is right, or has it evolved through a justification process of arguing that it is not wrong?
5. Do churches today have enough of the 1 Corinthians 12-13 qualities to practice the model suggested here? If so, give examples as exhibits to encourage others to follow. If not, what can be done to change the situation?
6. If you are perturbed by this chapter, analyze what parts of it were offensive and why. If you are sympathetic with the message of this chapter, analyze why you feel as you do.
7. What are the implications of question 6 if feelings divide along income or consumption lines?
8. In your opinion, should the basic unit of Christian action be the church or the individual?

7

The Model Illustrated

M any excellent examples of Christian community scattered
across the country could provide good case studies of the
model at work. I have chosen three real ones and one hypothetical
one to represent a varied selection of the qualities that make a
community of faith work.

The first story is of my own personal pilgrimage. Through
experience I have become convinced that the kingdom of God can
break through in economic matters and become the reference
point for all economic behavior. I do not live in a commune or
similar intentional community. I have a comfortable home in a
suburb of a major city. I have two children and a below-average
income for the community, but above-average income when compared with national standards. I offer my story partly to illustrate
that I am a fellow pilgrim in the search for responsible stewardship, not one who can speak from glowing success. My conviction
on these matters has kept me stewardship conscious, but in the
world of specifics, I find the applications difficult.

Perhaps my earliest recollection of the involvement of the
community of faith in the life of its people came when a farm accident disabled my father for a year. Many people in the church
were also farmers, and tractors and equipment descended on our
fields. In two days the entire corn crop was in storage. That was
followed by a blank check for labor from the Christian brothers
for any farm duties we could not handle ourselves. Our brothers
and sisters in the church responded spontaneously to the financial

emergencies that followed. Although it was a difficult year for us, I remember feeling that the church stood firmly between us and extreme financial uncertainty and despair. I learned through this experience that a community rather than a self-sufficiency orientation brings out the best in a church.

It is not yet completely clear to me how significant these early experiences were in my later thinking. This and similar examples of the Mennonite tradition of collective caring and sharing have made an indelible impression that will influence what I believe, teach, and do for the rest of my life.

Throughout high school and college, I had the advantage of not being rich, so it was easy for me to live in a manner consistent with my emerging feeling that the Christian calling involved a commitment to a more controlled lifestyle than the American dream entailed. On graduating from college, I bought the simplest economical new car on the market and took a job as a social worker in a medium-sized city.

Fortunately, there was a small, cohesive Mennonite fellowship there for me to relate to. The caring and sharing that had been collective now became much more personal. I felt myself responding to the fellowship not out of duty but out of love for my brothers and sisters. I adopted the norms that evolved within the church because of my desire to identify with the group and because I had, along with everyone else, a role in establishing the norms. It became clear to me that the legalism that accompanies large-scale collective caring can be replaced by an environment of personal caring and love from which group norms evolve. The community of believers willingly aspire to those norms because they want to be identified as members of the fellowship.

Two years later, when I left that community, I took along a vision of what a community of faith could become, although the economic issues of lifestyle and business practice had not been key concerns on which group norms had evolved. This was true perhaps because most of the members were young and did not earn incomes that allowed a resource-intensive lifestyle. I also married during my last year as a social worker, and lifestyle decisions became family decisions. My wife shared my basic stewardship ideas, but being on the same wavelength is not the same as agreeing on all the details.

Today I am not surprised that my occupational interests evolved from social studies to social work to economics. Somehow the cutting edge of every issue seemed to center on matters in the economic area of life. However, few voices within Christianity were speaking on economic issues. Most believers seemed all too ready to accept society's solutions to economic questions.

My graduate experience was significant not only because of what I learned in economics but also because of the association my wife and I had with a community of believers. That fellowship taught us much about what it means to live in God's kingdom. Again this church happened to be a fellowship in which the community tradition was historically rooted. From this base the functions of the church were carried out in numerous ways.

The festival of faith and worship occurred each Sunday with a wide range of participation. The intimacy of *koinonia* came through weekly meetings of a smaller subset of the congregation that entered into specific, mutual commitments to apply faith better. Regularly scheduled congregational business meetings provided a forum for collective administration in the church. Although the church had its share of weaknesses and shortcomings, it attempted to apply biblical teaching to all areas of life, including economic issues of lifestyle. In a general way it discouraged extravagance, but what was more important was the informal process by which extravagance was defined. Members who sought guidance on major purchases received the best input that those in the fellowship could give.

I well remember bringing our household budget to a koinonia group meeting where this information was shared by each one in hopes of providing support and guidance for future spending. I recall feeling the need to make some adjustments in our family spending pattern. Decisions arrived at in this manner are easier to carry out if friends can be depended on to encourage and challenge each other to meet their goals. The significant point of this experience is that economic decisions on lifestyle had become integrated into my expression of faith, and the fellowship of believers had accepted some degree of discerning and discipling function in this important area.

When I finished graduate studies and we had to make a choice regarding employment, the fellowship confirmed our feeling that we could serve God's kingdom better in the lower-paying of two alternative jobs, even though the higher-paying offer was tempting.

Two months after leaving that fellowship, my wife's youngest brother died in an automobile accident. On our way to the funeral, we spent an evening with the believers of that fellowship. They had gathered to share our grief, and their hurt was not superficial. We left for the funeral reassured that significant Christian love had been a part of our experience with that community of believers. Without that love, issues—particularly economic ones—become divisive and irritating.

Today the issues are less clear than they were in graduate school. We own a modest home by the standards of our town, but the county we live in is one of the more wealthy in the country. Furthermore, a good portion of the student body and the constituency of the school where I work are inclined to see a high-consumption lifestyle as God's blessing to them rather than as a dangerous obstacle to their faith and witness.

A congregation that believes in the dangers of materialism, a renewed joy in giving that comes from work on stewardship goals at the denominational level, a small group that attempts to practice the model I have described, and occasional involvement in inner-city churches in Chicago—these have convinced me that a believer must continue to swim upstream against the materialistic current of our time. It is not easy, but it can be a joy, not a burden. The process is slow and uncertain, but somewhere behind it all is an awareness that lifestyle and business practice are impor-

tant areas of concern for the church in twentieth-century America.
No Christian can take lightly decisions involving the world's
scarce resources.

This long personal story serves only to illustrate in a nontheo-
retical framework why I believe God's kingdom can break
through meaningfully in difficult areas of life. I also hope it will
make the model presented in the previous chapter seem more
plausible. But it cannot provide answers to other people's situations. In many ways the answers are not as important as the process because the questions change from year to year.

Economic Decision Making in Fellowship Groups

The next case is a hypothetical one using a congregation
named Alpha and a small fellowship group within it named Beta.
Alpha is a large, established congregation of 400 members, most
of whom attend regularly. It performs the functions of corporate
celebration of faith, group education, and Sunday worship. It
provides a social base for fellowship and has a strong collective
help program in the community and the world beyond. Alpha has
a paid minister and a committee structure that facilitates the fulfillment of these functions. It provides a superstructure for the
individual Christian to identify with and relate to on many issues.
But it teaches principles and general applications; in many ways it
is impersonal because of its size. Members know each other's
names and may visit each other's homes occasionally, but it is not
an intimate group in a personal sense.

Within Alpha is a subset of Christians who voluntarily gathered to work out some of the more specific applications of faith.
Beta formed not because members were disillusioned with Alpha
but because they realized that Alpha could not possibly serve all
of the biblical functions of the New Testament church. Beta consists of six families representing a cross-section of the congregation. Before joining together, they had gained mutual respect for
each other, developed from casual observation of each other's
participation in the church, so the members were not randomly

selected. They have in common a strong desire to grow spiritually and a belief that growth can best be achieved in the context of an intimate, caring group. They have committed themselves to each other as fellow disciples in the faith and have pledged to give a specific block of time each week for meeting. They also have covenanted together to share Christian love, support, and discipline in an attempt to work out more faithfully the teachings of Jesus in their social, economic, political, and physical environment.

Beta does not compete with Alpha. On doctrinal issues and the sacramental functions of the church, Alpha is the center for activity. If Beta has problems it cannot handle by itself, Alpha is the first resource it taps. Alpha is supported fully by all members of Beta, and Beta is seen as an instrument that can help carry out the full functions of the church.

The concern here is to explore Beta's activity in the economic area in hopes of seeing how some aspects of the model can be practiced. Financial issues were one of the last things Beta tackled, but when someone posed questions in this area, the members expressed themselves freely.

The issue arose when one couple (Jack and Alice Delta) made plans to purchase a new house. They asked for help in deciding the size and quality of house to build. The word from the Lord was extremely unclear to them. Jack said that he had $90,000 equity in his old house available for a down payment. His salary could easily allow payments on a mortgage of $130,000. The average home in the area where they lived was $90,000, but the new house they were considering was in an exclusive neighborhood where $220,000 was about average.

At first the group was excited about the possibility of the Deltas' new home, but then Jack asked what the group thought Jesus might advise if he were there. Here is the conversation that followed:

Jack: Last night I read in Matthew about the dangers of laying up treasures on earth. Would I be doing that?

Sam: Well, it is true that a house is essentially a consumption item in many ways.

Jack: At work they tell me it is a good investment, in other words, a sound financial move as well as good housing.

Sam: Nearly all realized appreciation on homes is put back into more expensive homes. This appreciation, which is the investment side of the purchase, never gets into productive investment where society at large benefits. It usually ends up encouraging even more consumption by placing people in bigger houses. Take the appreciation on your present home. Where is it going? Into better housing for you. But don't knock yourself. The tax laws almost force people to do this. Look at how God has blessed you! He has given you open doors. What are you waiting for?

Jack: All I need is the blessing of the community of faith. That's where you people come in. If Jesus is here, it is by his Spirit, who is imparted best in the context of this fellowship.

Joan: I haven't the faintest idea what to tell you, Jack. We will never have a decision like that to make ourselves because we can barely meet our rent each month, let alone save for a down payment. All I do is look at *Better Homes and Gardens* and dream what I'll do when I win a sweepstakes.

Diane: If there weren't so much poverty downtown and around the world, I'd feel much better about the whole idea.

Alex: Let's approach it this way: How much space and convenience do you need?

Alice: We would like a spare bedroom, and Jack needs a study at home. I would like a rough play area for the kids so the family room isn't such a mess when guests come. Our house now has room air conditioners that cool only part of the house, so central air would be a big help. Then there's the yard, which would sure beat the public park as a play area. Beyond that we need very little.

Alex: Do most of the rest of you feel these are needs a Christian should fulfill?

Joan: I would like all those things too, but the fact that I get along pretty well without them now makes me wonder if they are really needs. What do you think, Helen? Life hasn't been easy for you lately.

Helen: I don't know, Joan. Since Pete died and I had to begin a job, I've not been sure whether loneliness or lack of money is my bigger problem. I know that without some of you chipping in, I would never have made it. Anyway, at this point the kind of lifestyle Jack is talking about is so far from my thinking that I really can't give any advice offhand.

Sam: In my background, lifestyle questions were individual matters. Has that changed?

Jack: That was my experience too, Sam, but one reason why we got together as a committed group of believers was because we felt some of the existing patterns were not meeting our needs for spiritual growth. In my experience, the economic issues of life are my biggest spiritual blind spot.

Sam: You're right, Jack, but we obviously need more time and study to be of much help.

At this point the group resolved to prepare for careful Bible study on lifestyle matters, and Jack and Alice decided to hold off on their house building. The weekly meetings that followed were difficult. Some couldn't feel right about Deltas' proposed house as long as Helen was unable to have more than basic food and housing. Helen insisted that God would provide in his own time or had a reason for her unfortunate circumstances, and that Jack's decision was not related to her situation. Most did not agree with

Helen, saying that the body-of-Christ model implied that if Helen suffered, Jack suffered too.

Finally, around New Year's, the group decided to bring together their financial records of the past year. They included their earning and spending patterns, as well as their giving and investing. It was a long but fruitful evening. Everyone set consumption and charity goals for the new year. The group decided to take one meeting in June to check on the progress of the budgeting. They prayed that God would help them not to consume more than they ought and that he would provide in those cases where necessary consumption exceeded anticipated income, as was the case with Helen and a few others.

What happened? Did the Deltas build their big house? How many did not meet their goals? Did God provide for Helen, and if so, how? Those questions are for you to answer. All that can be said is that the process was carried through each year and, strangely enough, the range of consumption levels within the group became narrower, even though the income range did not. The members became more aware of resource use and its implications on lifestyle. The community of faith became a much more cohesive launching pad for its members.

Other groups formed within Alpha, and the congregation became a more dynamic testimony to the power of God in people's lives. However, all is not perfect in Alpha. Some say that too many restrictions are put on the lifestyle of some members because of the implicit expectations of the church. People have even left the church because of this. Others feel that the church is not disciplining enough because annual consumption goals are determined by individuals themselves, even if they do consult the counsel of their fellowship groups.

More recently, several businesspeople in the church have shared some business financial information with their small group. The group had little to offer at first, but the members eagerly learned about some of the business issues that are concerns of believing businesspeople. The process itself helped the business people maintain an awareness of the claims of Christ on their businesses, and it also helped the nonbusiness people in the group to gain a new appreciation for the way believers may influence others in their business dealings.

The exciting part was that the claims of the gospel were brought specifically to bear on economic decisions, alongside all the secular claims that bombard individuals. In other words, Jesus finally had a strong lobby working for him in the minds of his people, and it was making a difference.

Financial Counsel in Small Groups

The next two examples are true. They illustrate how some of the qualities of a community of faith can be applied in a simple setting without formal institutional trappings. Each case is told by a person involved in the story.

Case 1

For several years I have been part of a small fellowship that meets for breakfast once each week. We have met primarily for fellowship and mutual encouragement in the faith. The group consists of men with various educational backgrounds and vocations. Because we have relied on each other for feedback in the tough areas of faith, the fellowship has been a useful resource for establishing better accountability in our Christian life.

Personal finance has been a topic of frequent discussion. I recall one period when we were discussing the role of debt in managing our family budgets. Several in the group had been reading and thinking in this area and trying to relate the issue to biblical principles. Over several weeks we began, as individuals, to question the role of debt and its burden on the monthly budget. It seemed to us that a budget with little flexibility because of debt restricts freedom to give and leads to a spiritually unhealthy pre-occupation with material concerns. We especially questioned the use of debt to finance luxury items that depreciate in value.

The group is informal, and we make no attempt to force majority opinion on anyone. But in one instance, one of the men reevaluated his family's purchase of a fairly expensive travel van on credit. He felt that the burden of the monthly payments put an unnecessary strain on his budget. He also felt that the consumption of this luxury good had become a lesser value. He decided to sell the van, pay off the debt, and use the remainder of the proceeds to purchase a lower-cost vehicle for cash. Now, after two years, he looks back on the experience with a great deal of satisfaction and has on numerous occasions expressed his appreciation for the way in which our small breakfast fellowship has influenced his Christian life, even in resource use. I believe each of us could relate personal instances where our financial and vocational decisions have been shaped or altered because of insights gained from this group.

Case 2

The members of our church fellowship believe that Scripture says much about responsible stewardship. One example of how this belief was lived out occurred one year when a member wanted to buy a home for his family. While looking, the family realized that the obligation of a mortgage and the preoccupation of home ownership could detract from what they viewed as their real mission. Because of this, they sought the counsel of fellow believers to help in the decision.

When they found a house that seemed to fill their needs, they came and asked me to help them figure out whether the financial obligation of the house would fit their budget. "We will trust your judgment," they told me, "because you have more experience and expertise in these matters than we do."

I went over their income data and balance sheet and was concerned that the family was not in a position financially to purchase the house. Yet I knew they had invested so much time searching that backing out would be a disappointment. It was hard for me finally to tell them that I felt it was not wise to buy the house just then. I suggested that, for at least a year, they try to save the difference between their rent and the mortgage payments they would have made on the house. If they could do that, they would have both a better down payment and the confidence that they could meet the payments.

One year later the ideal house opened up a stone's throw from where they were renting, and they had the money to make the purchase. The house has served them well over the years, and the experience has confirmed in at least their minds and mine that God was at work in the economic areas of life. One by-product of the experience was that our trust and respect for each other deepened.

The Communal Option

The last case involves a different institutional structure from the previous examples. So far in this book there has been no mention of communes, in which a common treasury is used and discipling sometimes takes on an authoritarian tone. This has been deliberate for several reasons. First, most believers find those forms of religious and social organization so far removed from their experience that commune options appear irrelevant to them. Second, the Christian commune movement, which flourished in the 1960s and early 1970s, has gone through a period of re-evaluation and adjustment that has led to a substantial reduction in the numbers of believers who share common treasury experiences.

Perhaps the most stimulating case study of a communal experience is the book *Glimpses of Glory*, which describes the 30 year journey of Reba Place Fellowship in Evanston, Illinois.[1] This book is a candid look at the substantial benefits and costs of intense community life. From this experience at least four prerequisites for a successful common-treasury, intentional community experience stand out. First, each person involved must have a strong commitment to the group and to the idea that God can make it work. Second, each must be willing to accept the discipline of the elders or leaders when uniform decisions are required.

Third, a belief that service to God and others can be maximized more through a centralized community than through a decentralized congregational approach is important if communal living is to succeed. Fourth, the community family rather than the nuclear family unit must become the place where the pretenses of life are stripped away and security in social relationships develops.

Reba Place Fellowship began in 1957 with "a vision for 'being the church' in the city, a disciplined brotherhood which took discipleship seriously, including a common treasury and corporate decision making as a means of giving up self and seeking the will of God together.... The fellowship houses–as many as 15–were converted into extended family households of 12-24 persons, settings for support, lifestyle ministry, and intensive counseling."[2]

By 1987 the fellowship had evolved into a combination of households and cluster groups less focused on internal ministry and inner healing and more involved in mission outreach and service. Most members are not involved in the common treasury, but the concern for responsible stewardship is still important to members whether they are in the common treasury or manage their own family budgets.

The story of the thirty years of Reba Place history, as presented in *Glimpses of Glory*, is one of triumph and discouragement. God's grace and human frailty were brought together by a deep commitment that changed many lives. For Reba Place Fellowship, the economic component of community life is described in one section of a Vision Paper dated May 20, 1980, and called kingdom economics:

   –renouncing all to follow Christ
   –trusting that God will provide our economic needs, first
     through the Christian community
   –seeking first the Kingdom
   –working hard, praying, being good stewards of money and
     material resources

–investing in the Kingdom, giving generously, sharing income
and assets as much as possible, especially giving to the poor
–daily bread–minimizing storing up for the future and bor-
rowing against the future.[3]

There is evidence that these ideals were practiced in the fertile
soil of the intense communal experience of Reba Place Fellowship. There is also reason to believe that these values can continue
to guide the congregational members of Reba Place today who are
not in the common treasury.

It is a thesis of this book that Christians everywhere are
called to clarify the kingdom economics which should be lived out
in their lives, and that community life in some form is essential to
the clarification of values and the living process. Most will not
make dramatic plunges into communal forms of economic decision making, but the blessing that will result from adjustments on
the edges of our economic decisions might well open new doors of
witness and service. After all, it was only curiosity that started
Zacchaeus on his way to an enormous change in his economic
way of life (Luke 19:1-10).

Discussion Questions

1. Can you sketch the experiences that formed your view of the
   church? How important are other believers in the decision
   process when you make important choices?
2. If you were Jack and Alice, what would you do after the discussion described in this chapter?
3. Which of the following alternatives describes your feelings
   about this chapter?
   a. The model is not realistic for our society and does not fit
      my understandings of what Christians should do.
   b. This is an appropriate ideal model for Christians to work
      toward, but it is not likely to work in real life.
   c. This is an appropriate ideal model that Christians should
      apply in whatever ways they can.

4. Create your own list of kingdom economic values and contrast them with the Reba Place list.

5. Some people thrive in a communal experience while others find it oppressive. What accounts for these differences, and how should they be addressed by a community of faith?

8

Individual Freedom and Private Property: The First Pillar

The next four chapters discuss a few key, underlying ideas of the secular economic system of markets. These ideas together form a philosophy of the market economy. For now it is important to examine capitalism on its own terms and consider its viability as a social system for a secular society.

The bare essentials of a market economic system were touched on in chapters 1 and 2. The price system as an allocator, with its tie-in to production, has been discussed already. However, the mechanics of any system are meaningless apart from the ideas that undergird its operation. The ideology of market capitalism is closely tied to its practice and has important policy implications. How we think about the way the world works conditions our approach to policy. In other words, to relate effectively to markets, one must understand how they work and what ideology drives them. In this endeavor we venture beyond market mechanics and into the larger topic of market capitalism, which encompasses the social, philosophical, and historical dimensions of societal organization.

Building on the concept developed earlier of a price system of allocation, at least four components of a market environment form the social system often called capitalism. First is the concept of individual freedom, symbolized best in the institution of private property. Second is the view that social and economic harmony result if people, operating within defined rules of the game, pursue their own best interests, a concept considered in chapter 9. Third is belief in carefully defined limits on governmental intervention in the economy, an idea discussed in chapter 10. A fourth pillar of a capitalist order is the supporting noneconomic institutional framework that must complement the market activity. Each of these issues will be discussed at some length to illustrate the difficulty of simplistic conclusions about the positives and negatives of market capitalism.

Individual Freedom and Social Organization

Friedrich A. Hayek, a leading social theorist of this century, has done much to defend the view that individual freedom is essential to social organization.[1] Hayek, in contrast to less astute social thinkers who argue for freedom merely because it feels better than bondage, builds his understanding of natural liberty on the belief that social institutions and cultural characteristics are far too complex and historically rooted to be altered successfully by central planning. The belief that people created social institutions and therefore can alter them in socially beneficial ways is, in Hayek's view, incorrect.

If no blueprint went into the development of a social institution like language, for example, then no blueprint will effectively change that institution. The only goal of policy makers should be to structure rules that will prevent antisocial behavior, by which Hayek means behavior that hurts or coerces others.

Some of Hayek's examples are helpful in understanding this idea. In addition to language, which simply grew spontaneously over time without a designer, beehives and footpaths are examples of how society develops. Bees have orderly functions, and a hive can be a complex society, yet no hive is planned by a bright, intellectual bee. Footpaths develop as people walk from place to place because people independently find the same best route between two points and benefit by chance from each other's actions as the path hardens. Many a sidewalk builder has been frustrated when trying to plan where people should walk rather than building where they do. To carry this analogy further, society is better off if it engages only in rule making that puts necessary limits on behavior which hurts others. Prohibiting walkers from trampling someone's garden is appropriate, but designing the path is excessive social planning.

This spontaneous evolutionary development of the social order leads to the most desirable outcomes in economic life as well. Economic relationships are like footpaths. They evolve over time so that exchange arrangements develop which we call markets. Intervening in markets is like trying to build sidewalks where an architect, without full knowledge of walkers' preferences, would prefer them to be. The market intervention will be no more successful and probably as wasteful as the unused concrete sidewalks. The best economic policy protects property rights of market participants in the same way that the best sidewalk policy creates a rule against walking in gardens. Maximum freedom is retained, and optimal social organization can continue to evolve.

The manner in which markets contribute to desirable social organization should be explored further. When people are free to follow their interests and have exchangeable rights of ownership, opportunities for improvement become apparent. As long as people value items differently, there is a chance for both parties to gain from an exchange.

For example, suppose I win a car and you win a two-week cruise, but each of us would prefer the other's prize. If we exchanged prizes, both of us would be better off. If we never knew each other and made the exchange voluntarily through a middleman who made some profit on the deal, then all three parties would be better off. As long as each transaction is voluntary and ownership rights are clear, the gains are realized.

However, if the whole world had keys to the car and I had no title, the car would be nearly worthless to me in both use and exchange, since everyone would want it, even for trivial uses, it being free for the taking. The tragedy of this breakdown in property rights is that the car would only rarely be used for its most socially valuable purpose, since a doctor on an emergency call would have no more claim on it than would teenagers on a joy ride. Somehow, ownership must be assigned to someone who can prevent free use of the car.

But even if ownership is assigned to the teenagers, the doctor will use the car. Why? Because it is worth more to him than it is to them, and he will offer them something in exchange that they value more. This constant exchanging of things valued less for those valued more means that things are used by persons who value them more highly than anyone else. When all goods are being exchanged until that point is reached, the people as a group receive the greatest possible satisfaction of their wants. This, as Hayek and other market advocates see it, is the genius of markets.

In summary, the requirements for market success are as follows: First, property rights must be clearly defined. Second, exchange must be voluntary and unrestrained. Third, people must always seek their self-interest by trading wherever advantage can be found. The pursuit-of-self-interest concept will be explored in the next chapter. Here the topic is the necessity of clear property rights. The right to own property and exchange it freely links individual freedom and private property concepts together in an inseparable bond.

Concepts and Problems of Property Rights

Although the concept of property ownership is not difficult, its application can be controversial. For example, it is easy to measure a section of land, plant stakes, and claim ownership. In a world where the generation of wealth is land-based, the issue of private property results in minimal complication. However, suppose that, after the land is distributed, one person finds oil under his property. Assume also that the pool of oil extends under his neighbor's land. Who owns the oil? The answer isn't easy. Property rights in this case must be defined carefully, and how they are defined will make a big difference in how and when the oil is pumped. If property rights are not clarified, both landowners will likely pump as fast as they can to make sure they get their share, and the pumping will continue until the oil is gone. If generalized worldwide, the oil available will be used relatively rapidly and consumed at relatively low prices, unless property rights to the oil can be defined in ways that make it possible for owners to protect their oil from being taken.

This is only one sample of the difficulty of defining property rights. In fact, many property-rights issues today are not simple. Who owns the air space I live in? If I do, I can charge others for smoking or prohibit anyone from polluting my air. If no one owns it, everyone will use it freely and it will become unhealthy, since the prevailing opinion will be, "My tiny contribution to pollution cannot hurt the environment, so I might as well take the convenient way and pollute." In fact, property-rights cases are often ambiguous and difficult to enforce. Laws and rules on copyrights patents, water rights, space exploration, radio and television airwaves–all these are forms of property rights that have varying degrees of clarity and enforceability.

As the dominant factors of production shift from land and machinery to knowledge and intelligence (human capital), the definition of property rights becomes more obscure. Deciding at what point an idea or concept becomes proprietary and marketable is no small task. Enforcing the property right once it is assigned can create enormous problems as well. The speed of change, more than legal protection of designated property rights, has often been the factor that makes human capital marketable. For example, suppose you develop a new high-speed computer with revolutionary software. Being the innovator, you can reap the rewards before the imitators come out with clones. By that time you have a new idea and a new generation of computers that set the standard. In this case, the speed of change rather than a legal body effectively gives you property rights over your own intelligence.

Countries in the Eastern block are struggling with property-rights issues as they try to move toward capitalism. In an effort to privatize the producing and consuming sectors, they have distributed vouchers (credits or money for people to purchase ownership), conducted auctions of property, returned assets to previous owners who can be found, or simply advertised property for sale. None of these attempts is free of complications, and the process of privatization is going slowly. It is no easy task to assign property rights.

Rights are finally assigned, however, by whatever governmental group is responsible for their definition. As a rule they reflect the prevailing values present in a society at any given time. Some have suggested that a 100 percent inheritance tax be enacted to prevent concentrations of property rights and so to give each generation a fair start in the economic race. Others support different kinds of tax and transfer programs that distribute resource claims according to some definition of justice. At least, it must be recognized that many claims are made on property that is not earned. Thus, values other than productivity become important considerations in distribution of property rights.

Indeed, there is a movement toward increased redefinition of property rights by those who favor particular social outcomes. The freeing of slaves over a century ago was an obvious example of achieving social goals by redefining property rights. Distinctions between property-rights policies and social-planning policies become less clear as society becomes more complex and more sophisticated at shifting property rights. In the United States and Canada, the legislative and judicial functions of government constantly define and redefine property rights in an effort to clarify ownership and make the market process of exchange more fair. Unfortunately, we are becoming a society where litigation has become so rampant that the courts and legal profession capture a sizable portion of the gains realized from clarified property rights.

Another difficulty with determining property rights is that they can be held as absolute or qualified rights. An absolute right gives persons title to the property in question, the right to use the property as desired and keep what they produce with it, the right to sell the property claim, and the right to destroy the property if they so desire. Many situations exist where some but not all of these attributes are part of the property right. You may have certain rights to a river, but you are limited in what you can do with it. You may own land but are not allowed to build a factory on it. Nearly every right has qualifications, which means that the application of property rights is seldom absolute.

Recently my father chose to sell his small farm by subdividing the land into a few lots. It took several years, a large retention pond, multiple surveying expeditions, drainage studies, a bicycle path extension to the highway, permit applications (to state, county, and township bodies), and more than $50,000 to pay for all this before he was allowed to sell any property. Apparently governmental units thought it was necessary to limit dad's property rights for the public benefit.

The biblical concept of ownership was far from absolute, because only God was the absolute owner. "The earth is the Lord's and all that is in it, the world, and all those who live in it" (Ps. 24:1). This claim is a theme throughout the Bible. The right to use and keep the output of property was about as far as ownership extended in the Old Testament (Lev. 25). The right to sell property more freely seems to be part of the New Testament context.

In summary, property ownership is important not as an absolute value designed to testify to individual autonomy but as a vehicle to serve goals important to human well-being. The capitalist view is that the more carefully and completely property rights are spelled out, the better off society will be. This assumes that an accepted view of justice guides those who determine what the rights are and that free exchange of those rights is possible.

Challenges to Property Rights

For some Christians the notion of private property seems to violate a sense of justice and the natural order of creation. Those who share that view frequently draw on the writings of earlier Christians who argued for common property as the best way to foster social harmony. One such writer was John Chrysostom, a fourth-century preacher who argued that private property is not the Christian way to organize society:

> Mark the wise dispensation of God! That he might put mankind to shame, he has made certain things common, as the sun, air, earth, and water...whose benefits are dispensed equally to all as brethren.... Observe that concerning things that are common there is no contention, but all is peaceable.... But when one attempts to possess himself of anything, to make it his own, then contention is introduced, as if nature herself were indignant, that when God brings us together in every way, we are eager to divide and separate ourselves by appropriating things, and by using those cold words 'mine and thine.' Then there is contention and uneasiness. But where this is not, no strife or contention is bred. This state therefore is rather our inheritance, and more agreeable to nature.[2]

In this example, Chrysostom builds his case against private property on a faulty observation. He picks his examples of common goods from items not scarce in his day, and selects scarce goods as evidence that people fight when private goods are allowed. In fact, the conflict occurred because of scarcity, not because of property rights. This mistake is common even in modern analyses of property claims. What Chrysostom did not understand is that if common property becomes scarce, a great deal of hostility can result, and the property in question probably will not be put to its best use.

A more helpful Christian perspective on property rights comes from the recognition that property rights and income are closely related. Wages come from the ownership of labor. Interest is a return on capital. Rent derives from land ownership. Thus income distribution is closely tied to ownership patterns in an economy. Altered distribution patterns can result from changing ownership claims as well as from income-transfer programs. Since constant redefinitions of ownership are required in a dynamic system, there may be creative ways that poor people can be helped without the difficulties sometimes associated with income transfer programs. The effort to help employees gain ownership in their company is one example of using claims on property to achieve a social goal of redistribution.

In Western culture, individual freedom means far more than the right to own and exchange goods and ideas. The Bill of Rights to the U.S. Constitution lists other expressions of freedom that affect all of life, but none would mean much if property and exchange rights of the individual are unprotected. This emphasis of individual freedom is quite different from the biblical content of property rights described in chapter 3. In that chapter property arrangements were weighted more heavily by income and wealth distributional goals then is true in society at large today.

Once property rights are defined in a capitalistic system, the economy proceeds as people pursue their self-interest in the markets where property rights constantly are exchanged. The next chapter explores the nature of this self-interest.

Discussion Questions

1. Do you see voluntary exchange markets as natural developments in the evolution of social organization, or as a construction of thinkers who have had their ideas implemented?
2. From Scripture, can you develop the case for individual autonomy and freedom? If so, how? If not, where does the case come from?
3. If the right to own the *product* of property rather than the property itself is at the center of biblical property-rights teaching, what implications does that have for modern property-rights arrangements?

9

The Harmony of
Self-Interested Behavior:
The Second Pillar

A second topic important to a proper understanding of markets is the way the institutions of a society cope with the
people's egocentric nature. At first glance it would seem that if
everyone pursued what pleased themselves, social harmony would
deteriorate. Yet the system of market capitalism argues the opposite, given certain prerequisites in the social order.

The prerequisites have been touched on at various places already, but they can be listed as follows: property rights must be
clearly defined and enforceable, society must permit and protect
free exchange, and a price system must be the dominant guide for
resource allocation. In light of these requirements, some observations arise about the nature of self-interest and how it will be expressed.

Clearly it must be restrained to some extent, or the first two
requirements will be threatened. If I think it is in my interest to
interfere with your property rights or to coerce you into an exchange you do not want, then something must prevent me from
exercising my will over you. In most cases the laws of the land, if
properly enforced, are sufficient to deter me from infringing on
your rights. Thus, if people are law-abiding and pursue their
greatest advantage in market exchanges, society will attain its

highest possible level of satisfaction of want. This is the theory of market capitalism. Since exchanges occur in every area of life, including the social, political, and religious areas, social harmony need not be considered a narrow economic term. Both the economics of love and marriage and public-choice theory use market considerations to analyze human relationships.

However, social relationships are enormously complex, and human nature is inclined to find and exploit any loophole in property rights definitions for personal gain. Therefore, the idea that social harmony can be brought about by proper institutional arrangements requires an optimism about social progress that not everyone shares. In fact, the social harmony of the market system is little more than a statement that things get done about as well as one might expect them to get done, given the complexity of the world. It says almost nothing about how people feel about the relationships that result from market activity. It does not consider the plight of those with almost nothing to exchange in the market. It has no way of sorting out what is fair, even though a perception of fairness is essential for the survival of a social group. In fact, an entire society could deteriorate and lose its viability even if it had markets operating efficiently.

In short, long-term social harmony requires a particular kind of self-interested behavior. Three types of self-interest will be explored to see how compatible they are with market capitalism.

Mandeville and Narrow Self-Interest

The first type of self-interest could be called the narrow view. According to this view, people function in a pain-and-pleasure framework in which any behavior that brings more pleasure than pain will be chosen. Life is enjoyed most when people engage in activities that produce the greatest net pleasure, so they choose those activities to fill the day. Apart from pain and pleasure, moral restraint is irrelevant. Thus a person would rob banks if there was no chance of being caught and the loot brought more pleasure than could be earned in honest labor.

Such a narrow view of self-interest is presupposed in some critiques of capitalism. This is not surprising, because economists usually discuss human behavior with models assuming that people are individualists who maximize their pleasure.

One philosopher who influenced early thought about the nature of capitalistic self-interest argued facetiously that the system would work for the common good no matter how evil or self-centered an individual was. Bernard Mandeville (1670-1733), in *Fable of the Bees,* painted parallels between a beehive and human society.

> Thus every Part was full of Vice,
> Yet the whole Mass a Paradise: . . .
> The Root of Evil Avarice,
> That damn'd ill-natur'd baneful Vice,
> Was Slave to Prodigality,
> That noble Sin; whilst Luxury
> Employ'd a Million of the Poor,
> And odious Pride a Million more;
> Envy it self, and Vanity,
> Were Ministers of Industry;
> Their darling Folly, Fickleness,
> In Diet, Furniture and Dress,
> That strange ridic'lous Vice, was made
> The very Wheel that turn'd the Trade.
> Their Laws and Clothes were equally
> Objects of Mutability;
> For, what was well done for a time,
> In half a Year became a Crime;
> Yet while they alter'd thus their Laws,
> Still finding and correcting Flaws,
> They mended by Inconsistency
> Faults, which no Prudence could foresee.[1]

This statement, which suggests that the proper system could turn evil into benefit, virtually enshrines the *laissez-faire* system as the redeemer of the selfish or evil bent in people. Even the most heinous person will end up unintentionally serving the common good. This notion was questioned by a group of Russian faculty during recent curriculum development meetings in Moscow where I was a consultant. Someone from the American team of advisors had made the comment that capitalism was made for sinners because it neutralized the harmfulness of self-interest. The Russians seemed to feel that Mandevillian self-interest could flourish to the social detriment if markets were free. I shared the Russian view that only in a perfectly constructed society could this narrow self-interest produce social good. Today Russians are finding out how socially undesirable the expression of Mandevillian self-interest can be when freedom is extended in a society that is far from perfectly constructed for markets.

If capitalist society really depended on this Mandevillian kind of self-interest, it would deteriorate quickly into a police state or anarchy. In reality, capitalism requires something more than this narrow self-interest. Property rights will be impossible to enforce unless people have some respect for the rights of others or an appreciation of the golden-rule (Matt. 7:12) concept that limits their individual pursuit of pleasure. One refrains from robbing a bank because of an inner sense that it is wrong to do so, not only because of the fear of being caught. If that moral sense is lacking in a culture, society cannot preserve its people's freedom. The success of the voluntary tax system, the existence of self-service gas pumps, and the fact that cars still have hub caps all testify to the reality of moral restraint in society that supersedes narrow self-interest. The increase in tax fraud and the need for locks of all kinds, however, testify to the decline of the moral fabric of society.

A Russian ethicist made the sad observation that there is no ethical standard which would compel a motorist to pay a self-service gas station attendant if leaving the station with a tank full of gas could be done without detection. It is hard to see how markets can move ahead until the environment for the pursuit of self-interest is more fully developed.

Another way of stating the issue is to say that the preservation of property rights becomes so difficult in a society without a built-in moral restraint that auction or market activity ceases to be effective and desirable. Mandeville's belief that the system will neutralize the evil and turn it into good is not a satisfactory explanation of how society can survive and prosper.

Smith and Benign Self-Interest

Adam Smith (1723-1790) offered a more plausible explanation of how the pursuit of self-interest could lead toward social harmony. In *The Theory of Moral Sentiments,* Smith developed the idea of *moral sympathy,* which he posited as the key ingredient in successful social organization. This sympathy consists of a person's desire for social approval and, therefore, his willingness to evaluate his behavior from the vantage point of a disinterested third party. This vantage point allows for more objective moral judgments by pushing aside personal bias and greed. True self-interest involves this quality of sympathy and provides a built-in moral dimension lacking in Mandevillian narrow self-interest. To Smith, humanity is basically good, and the exercise of self-interest is really the practice of behavior approved by impartial moral judgment.

Smith's second and far more prominent book is *An Inquiry into the Nature and Causes of the Wealth of Nations.* This massive work describes how the pursuit of self-interest, restrained by moral sympathy and the appropriate institutional framework, works toward the common good as if an "invisible hand" were guiding the process. Smith, working in the eighteenth century, wrote of the entrepreneur:

By preferring the support of domestic to that of foreign industry, he intends only his own security; and by directing that industry in such a manner as its produce may be of the greatest value, he intends only his own gain, and he is in this, as in many other cases, led by an invisible hand to promote an end which was no part of his intention. Nor is it always the worse for the society that it was no part of it. By pursuing his own interest he frequently promotes that of the society more effectually than when he really intends to promote it.[2]

For Smith, the "invisible hand" that guided economic activity toward harmonious ends was helped along by the moral sense described as "sympathy." In other words, market economies needed to have a moral or "sympathetic" base before the common good could be served by the pursuit of individual self-interest. It is generally believed that this view of benign self-interest, carefully articulated in the earlier *Theory of Moral Sentiments,* is an important part of *The Wealth of Nations,* even though it is not stated as clearly in the later work. This view requires that people have interdependent preference patterns rather than independent ones. Choices are made based on others' viewpoints and values. Contemporary microeconomic behavior modeling has not effectively incorporated this interdependency and therefore has missed the richness of Smith's observations.

Rawls and Justice

Higher levels of morally guided behavior would result from the application of a Rawlsian analysis of justice. John Rawls (1921–) has suggested that *appropriate moral behavior* produces what an unbiased observer would prescribe for a society.

For example, assume that you are about to be born at a randomly selected spot in the world. Would you choose to take a gamble and hope for the slim chance of landing in a first-world country rather than the more likely probability of a third-world situation? Or would you prefer to redistribute wealth enough to reduce the probability of starving if you landed in a third-world country? If you would choose the latter, then Rawlsian justice requires that the same judgment be made by a person already born in a desirable location. People who feel that way should promote some redistribution of income or wealth in their current situation.

Rawls's "veil of ignorance" is similar to Smith's sympathy. The pursuit of self-interest must be conditioned by a detached, unbiased moral quality if it is to produce social harmony.[3]

Religious Restraint on Behavior

Most religions of the world have an even higher level of moral restraint governing human behavior because they often assume human depravity. Judeo-Christian history, from the sin of Adam and Eve and on through Scripture, dramatizes the idea that humans have a tendency to destroy harmony rather than create it unless God redeems people from selfish preoccupations. The Islamic faith also prescribes many social and religious restraints against self-oriented pursuits. Sacrifices, penance, forgiveness, and purification rites are common in most religions as safeguards against destructive self-interested behavior.

Social harmony is generally considered to be possible only if individuals have a religious experience of some kind that focuses their goals on the well-being of others. Only in the service of God and others can one truly increase social harmony. This transcendent self-interest is foolishness to those who are not believers. For this reason, religious people often are not optimistic that the world will progress toward social harmony without a religious experience.

The question that is important here is whether a system like capitalism can flourish without a Christian solution to selfishness. Can the pursuit of self-interest by individuals be self-regulating so that social harmony can prevail?

Two comments seem appropriate. First, if the pursuit of self-interest occurs in a context where the individual has power to limit the choices of others, then social harmony is not likely to occur spontaneously. Second, if no such position of power is present, then social harmony can result if a Smithian or Rawlsian moral sense predominates, but not if a Mandevillian approach to self-interested behavior is common.

Some economists have used the term *selfishness* to speak of the Mandevillian view and the term *self-interest* to comment on the Smithian or Rawlsian view of social harmony. The special compassion and love that Christians are to share may help society move from selfish to self-interested behavior and therefore to social viability, but thus far compassion and love has not dominated social relationships within society at large.

Although this self-interested rather than selfish behavior may lead toward social harmony, it is not a sufficient condition to sustain that harmony. In order for the economic system to have permanence, it must produce conditions perceived to be fair by the people of a society. This perception of fairness is far more important than is commonly thought. If people feel that society treats them unfairly, they sometimes resort to narrow self-interest and feel justified in doing so. Decisions to steal will be based on probabilistic cost-benefit analysis, and much of the order of society will disappear. Ultimately, a majority of the public will demand authoritarian control over this kind of behavior, and the glue that holds together a free society will disintegrate. When a nation fails to deal with perceptions of unfairness in its public policy, it jeopardizes its people's freedom. In these matters, perceptions are often as important as realities.

The increase in income disparities and the related decay of American cities are two factors testing social harmony in the country today. The perception that something is not fair is, no doubt, part of the cause of increased crime and the loss of social solidarity in communities. More jails and increased punishments will merely feed the perception. Without a dialogue on fairness and a conscious effort to achieve specific goals in that area, there will be limited social harmony no matter how diligently people pursue their self-interest in the marketplace. Efficiencies promised by the market will be squandered in maintaining law and order until fairness is perceived to exist. This is not to say that those crying "foul" have a good case. It is simply true that when fairness and justice issues are not a part of the public discourse, accepted standards of fairness cannot evolve. Unfortunately, free-market rhetoric often bends discussion away from moral discourse because it is erroneously assumed that the market distribution is efficient and therefore good.

In short, the pursuit of self-interest can have positive effects on the social glue of a society if it is guided by a Smithian or, ideally, a Christian moral framework. Behavior guided by narrow self-interest and devoid of a moral reference point ultimately will destroy freedom in society. Perceptions of unfairness, when widespread, undermine social solidarity and lead to behavior that can only be contained by an authoritarian police state. History has not yet proved whether secular societies can maintain a moral framework sufficient to protect a social order governed by self-interest. The final verdict is not yet in on the viability of self-interest as a route to harmony. That verdict will depend upon whether the people of a nation feel they have a fair chance in life. If they believe that they do, then the system will be viewed as legitimate and will endure.

Power and Control in an Economy

Because a morally controlled, powerless self-interest is needed for social harmony in society, it is important to explore a bit further the nature of power and control in a market economy. Governmental authority is one source of control that can create unfairness and perceptions of unfairness. (This issue will be treated in the next chapter.) The other major source of control in society is in the private sector, where concentrations of productive assets can lead to power and influence. We can see how control destroys social solidarity by examining two different situations in economic life.

The first is the farmer who makes his livelihood by selling milk to a dairy. His neighbor, who is also a dairy farmer, is a close friend; the two share many things, including tips on how to get more milk from their herds. When one has a misfortune, the other helps. Each pursues his self-interest, but self-interest and close friendship are not mutually exclusive to these farmers, even though they are in the same business. Neither feels that the other has power to manipulate him in a way that will make him worse off.

The second situation is in Detroit, where General Motors and Ford are neighbors. Both are in the same business, but they share a totally different relationship than the farmers. General Motors is secretive with its new inventions, and its personnel rejoice when Ford has a setback. Rivalry and disharmony are more apparent than social solidarity between these two producers. Each believes the other has the power to damage its business.

Why are these two situations so different? The answer lies not in the absolute size or type of business but in the *perception* that the parties have of each other. Compared to the total milk market, the farmers are such small operators that they cannot set their own prices for milk or cow feed. They simply take the prices which the market dictates. Since neither farmer's operation will hinder the other's business, they have nothing to lose and everything to gain by pulling for each other. The result is social harmony brought about by a market structure in which the operators cannot influence the market for their benefit and their neighbor's detriment.

The auto industry in Detroit is completely different. There, by changing production levels, General Motors or Ford can influence the prices of cars. When one increases its share of the market, the other usually loses sales. Consequently, an intense rivalry builds as each side jockeys for greater market share. The same situation might exist in a small town where only two auto mechanics or two medical doctors work. The point is that if any producer has a large share of the sales in a market and the entry of new firms is unlikely, then that producer is viewed as having control over others even if choosing to be generous. The perception can be more important to others' behavior than the reality.

This perception, whether true or not, creates an environment where consumers and laborers feel helpless. Mistrust leads to the formation of organizations with countervailing power that can increase waste and reduce efficiency. Huge corporate entities are not suspect as much for what they do as for what they represent. In fact, they have generated unprecedented quantities of goods and services at relatively reasonable prices. However, they sometimes are unable to gain consumers' and workers' trust and consequently rank low in social respect.

When some people appear to have power and control over others, some deterrent must restrict their exercising that power if it is real. If the power of the corporation is not real but merely perceived, then some intangible factor must convince the powerless that they will not be exploited. Whether the power is real or only perceived, the factor that keeps mistrust in check is the recognition that a moral restraint guides the corporation's decision processes. Without this factor in the social consciousness, society cannot thrive in the long run. Paul Heyne, commenting on the problem of inflation, notes, "If people come to believe that they're being defrauded, they will more readily throw off the constraints of ethics and do unto others what they think is being done unto them." [4]

In summary, "moral sympathy," a veil of ignorance, or golden-rule thinking should condition the behavior of participants in an economy if that economy is to be considered fair and therefore viable in the long run. This kind of moral restraint reduces the costs of ensuring free exchange and minimizes the mistrust of power that can threaten a system which includes large, concentrated units of production.

Discussion Questions

1. Is this chapter saying any more than that society will be viable in the long run if people respect each other?
2. Is Christianity required to give society a moral framework, or can humanitarian goodwill, feelings of solidarity within soci-

ety, or commonsense wisdom be sufficient to sustain the moral fabric of society?

3. Economists of our day frequently ignore the philosophical and moral dimensions of people's efforts to maximize their pleasure. Why do you suppose this is true? (This is a hard question requiring some understanding of the methods economists use in their work.)

10

Limited Government Activity: The Third Pillar

Thus far we have explored two important ingredients of a market system: the institution of private property and the pursuit of self-interest as a harmonizing force in society. Neither is a simple concept because both interact with other areas of social organization.

The third key ingredient of market capitalism is the concept of *laissez-faire*, or hands off with respect to regulation by the government. This idea that government must have a limited and clearly specified role in economic activity is not simply based on a dislike or mistrust of public officials or a belief that nonprofit-related activity is inefficient. Rather, it comes out of the eighteenth-century worldview that was discussed briefly in chapter 1. During that century the concept of a system took shape in a new way. Isaac Newton discovered that the universe functioned as a giant machine governed by internal forces that continued in endless repetition. Human interference with these forces could only cause problems since collective human choice is not as systematic as the natural order itself.

The disciplines of physics, chemistry, and biology began to perceive the world in a systematic, self-contained fashion. Indeed, creation was viewed as a beautifully designed machine that functioned in a self-perpetuating and organized manner. God was usually praised as an ingenious Creator, but was considered to be an absentee landlord who did not become involved in the operation of the world. This deistic religious orientation is prominent in the writings of many influential people of this period, often called the Enlightenment.

It is not surprising that the social sciences began to seek answers to social problems in the same manner. Finding systematic patterns of behavior that could be documented and generalized into laws became the method of the social scientist as well as of the physical scientist. Economics, more than most social sciences, followed this pattern of understanding how the world works. In the work of Adam Smith and the other classical economists, an interrelated, systematic economic and social order was spelled out. The market-price system, with its great powers of coordinating economic activity, became the economic orthodoxy of the late eighteenth century. Like the internally balanced machine of the physical sciences, economics was thought to be a self-perpetuating system that could not benefit from outside tinkering.

No longer were governmental bodies thought capable of improving things with policy interventions. In fact, intervention of almost any kind was thought likely to harm the proper functioning of the market. People acting through government were seen as tinkerers outside the system rather than as part of its internal balance. The natural involvement of people was to be only as individual competitors pursuing their own self-interest. Thus a hands-off policy with respect to government became part of classical economic orthodoxy. Much of this positivistic worldview is retained by economists and businesspeople today.

However, few people are anarchists. Most recognize that government is necessary for certain functions, even in a free-market environment. Thus, the debate focuses not on whether government is needed but on what kind of governmental involvement is appropriate in a free-market system. The following section describes four areas of government involvement often thought appropriate for a free economy.

Rules of the Game

The first and most obvious function of government in economic life is the establishment of the rules of the economic process. Although many of the economic rules are spelled out in the constitution and the laws of a society, some specific economic rules are needed. The constitution guarantees such things as freedom of speech and assembly, rights of minorities, and rights of the accused. The laws that pertain most directly to economic life are those defining property rights and the exchange process. This requires executive and judicial functions of government. As discussed earlier, the task of defining these rights is complex and somewhat arbitrary. For more conservative economists, the task of assigning property rights is the main economic function of government. If ownership of all resources is properly assigned, then the participants in a system can come to the auctions of the world to exchange their goods, services, and property claims so that efficiency will be maximized.

For example, if a river can take a hundred tons of effluent and still be ecologically safe, the government can auction off a hundred units of polluting rights. Those whose waste is hard to clean up will outbid those who can clean up their effluent more easily. Those who purchase the rights to pollute will be allowed to dump effluent in the river. Efficiency and ecology will be served because the river is still healthy and the amount of effluent it can process comes from polluters who would have the highest cleanup costs. This is true because every potential polluter will bid for the right to pollute to the point where it is cheaper to clean up its pollution instead. The winning bidders would have still higher alternative cleanup costs.

In this way, virtually everything that is not truly free can be allocated. Governments must still determine how to package the property rights and develop the necessary means to enforce the rights once they are exchanged in the market. But the issue of who owns them becomes a purely economic matter, with the dominant value being efficiency or lowest-cost concerns. The most common alternative method would be to have the government retain ownership of the river and simply decide whom it will allow to pollute or to restrict everyone's pollution no matter what the cost may be to polluters.

In addition to property rights determination, governments must make rules to maintain order in markets. Antitrust rules are designed to prevent producers from joining forces to exert monopoly power against consumers. Health and safety laws protect the consumer and worker. Civil-rights laws are meant to protect minorities from discrimination in the labor market. Consumer-protection laws seek to prevent fraud against consumers. Numerous government commissions interpret and enforce an elaborate array of rules designed to make economic relationships fair and efficient.

Some people view these efforts at regulation as futile attempts by bureaucrats, who tend to seek their own goals of power and income rather than the public good. Thus governmental rule-setting that takes the form of coercive regulation becomes license to establish a massive bureaucracy with goals of its own. If the electorate is unable to express its wishes effectively, and if private and public interests diverge, then this form of rule-making will fall short of its intentions and may be counterproductive. People with this view generally oppose government rule-making that comes in the form of regulation. The dangers of private monopolies or consumer fraud concern them less than the dangers of government regulatory power. Others argue that an informed electorate with conscientious public servants can establish effective rules that will make economic markets perform as desired. A free press will be the competition that government will have to face.

Stabilization Policy

Most people in capitalistic societies today expect their governments to provide an environment for full employment without inflation. Governments have struggled to achieve this goal since the 1930s with varying degrees of success. The two general tools used to reach the goals are called monetary and fiscal policy.

Monetary policy is a simple concept with extremely complex institutional applications. Picture what would happen if someone stuffed $100 into the pocket of every buyer at a given auction. Unless the goods for sale increased proportionately in volume, buyers would bid prices higher. If money were taken from the bidders, prices would fall. When money is scarce relative to goods and services, its value rises and more goods can be bought with each dollar because prices fall. Conversely, when money is plentiful relative to goods and services, its value falls and less can be bought with it because prices are high. In short, the amount of money in a society has a significant impact on prices and output, and many economists believe it is desirable to keep the money supply at a level that encourages growth but, at the same time, prevents pressure for price changes.

In order to keep track of the money supply, most societies give government control over it, including the power to create and define money and make legal-tender laws. In the United States, the Federal Reserve Board (FED) manages the money supply through the banking system.

Whether the FED is capable of regulating the money supply successfully is a question around which much controversy exists. The difficulty becomes apparent when one realizes what the auction bidders might choose to do with the extra $100 that they have in their pockets. Some may choose to keep a good portion of it as pocket money and not spend as much as others at the auction. Since the extra money in the system will lower interest rates and therefore the cost of holding money, some may choose to hold additional cash that they otherwise would have invested in interest-earning alternatives. In short, money intended to stimulate buying and selling activity, thereby reducing unemployment, will still be idle. This is simply because people desire to hold more money, and so the monetary policy of the FED does not work.

The FED pulls money out of the economy if it fears inflation more than unemployment. Both pumping money in and pulling it out are precarious ventures with uncertain outcomes and long time lags between action and results. Consequently, some believe the effort is not worth trying and may even be counterproductive.

The role of the FED in helping to create the national debt is also part of monetary policy. When the treasury of the government needs to borrow money, it pays whatever interest rate is required to find lenders. This effort to borrow for government projects may cause interest rates to rise, so the FED might simply create the money for the treasury to spend. Interest rates need not go up as much in the short run if this happens, but the treasury can then enter the market for goods and services with the new (inflationary) money and drive up prices by its debt-financed buying.

Because of this temptation to expand the money supply too rapidly, some suggest that, to restrain inflation, a precious metal like gold should back each currency unit. This restraint on inflation would rely on natural forces limiting gold extraction and refining rather than on the ability of people to make sound judgments in the face of short-run political and economic pressures. Unfortunately, adopting the gold standard does not eliminate the human element because people must either fix the rate for exchanging gold and currency or face a market rate that might fluctuate wildly. It is impossible to know in advance whether long-run monetary and economic stability would ever result from a gold standard, but the risks of finding out could be substantial. Despite the controversies over how government should handle monetary policy, there is widespread agreement that government must play some function in promoting a stable currency system.

Fiscal policy is the other major stabilization policy tool. It is concerned with the influence of taxation and government spending on the overall economy. In the past, tax cuts and spending increases were thought to stimulate the economy toward more rapid growth, while tax increases and spending reductions were expected to pull the economy back from inflation. In the 1960s and early 1970s, these tools seemed to be effective aids to economic stability. More recently, with increasing sophistication of the citizens, better availability of information, and an inflationary economy that generates certain expectations, the policy tools of the earlier decades seem less helpful. Nevertheless, macroeconomic policy, as the stabilization plan is called, continues to be a central governmental function in the economy as it taxes, spends, and changes the money supply. The intricacies of stabilization policy will not be developed in this book. Any text on the principles of macroeconomics dedicates several hundred pages to this task.

Public Goods and Neighborhood Effects

A third function of government relates to types of economic activity that the market is not well suited to perform. To understand this problem, one might ask why those strongly opposed to government provision of bread seem quite willing to have the government run a tornado-warning system. The answer becomes clear after examining the different natures of bread supply and storm-warning devices. Buyers of bread can receive the full benefits of the bread when they eat it. However, suppose that when one person ate bread, everyone in the community received nourishment. In this case, everyone would benefit from one person's purchase, so everyone would wait for someone else to buy. Consequently, less food would be consumed than the population desired.

Although this example seems absurd, it has many similarities to the provision of storm-warning devices. In fact, everyone will benefit if one person successfully installs a warning system for himself. Thus, the market will provide no warning system since everyone will hope to have someone else provide the service which everyone else can then hear for free. Seeing this dilemma, citizens join forces and require everyone to pay their share through taxes. In other words, government provides the service so there will be no free riders.

Economists have terms that describe this situation. They say that warning devices have *externalities* or *neighborhood effects* that the market cannot capture. The expression *neighborhood effects* will be used in this book because it describes quite well what is happening in areas where goods or services benefit even those who choose not to purchase them. These goods and services are called *public goods*. Clearly, a storm-warning system is that kind of service. A pure public good can be provided to additional people in the system at little or no additional cost once it is provided for some. In the case of bread, when a family gets bigger, the amount of bread required for consumption increases because two family members cannot consume the same bread. However, when a few new families move into town, it is not necessary to increase the number of sirens because the new citizens benefit from the same sirens that protect continuing residents. This important distinction is overlooked by those inclined to determine what government should provide based on some emotional distrust of its role in the economy.

Many public goods could be listed and evaluated for their public goods qualities. Some have qualities that only partially fit the public goods definition, so it is easy to understand why so much public controversy can exist regarding government's role in providing them. One example is illustrated by a controversial case.

Public education long has been provided by governments at the local level. Most agree that it is more desirable to live in an educated rather than an illiterate society. When you learn to read, I benefit because you move through checkout lines faster, observe stop signs better, vote more sensibly, and in general, are more interesting to be around. Yet, if you pay for all of your education, I get all those benefits free. True, you can keep some of the benefits to yourself, because you need not share the after-tax income you receive as a result of your reading skills. Still, we have a partial public good, and most Western societies have chosen to provide at least some education through the public sector. Some argue that we should simply require everyone to get an education and let private sources provide it. Either way, government intrudes into the market in an effort to remedy the neighborhood effects of education.

The list of similar goods and services is lengthy, and each citizen must judge whether the neighborhood effects of the item are sufficient to merit some kind of government intervention. Other markets where government provision is widely used because of these neighborhood effects in consumption include health care, national defense, retirement planning, police and fire protection, communications, transportation, and garbage collection. Although there are many different and creative ways of helping the market process to work, it is clear that the market, by itself, would misallocate these items.

This extended discussion of public goods is only the beginning of a complete look at circumstances where the market cannot function properly by itself. Neighborhood effects exist not only in the consumption of certain items but also in the production of some goods and services. The market process may well be much more distorted in how it generates cost information for producers than most people realize. The continuing degeneration of the earth provides evidence that that many economies are not counting the full cost of their production processes when they produce. Industrial bidders for resources may be paying adequately for labor, capital, and some resources, but they are paying far too little for nonrenewable resources and the land, water, and air they use and damage in the production process.

The true cost of producing corn, for instance, includes far more than the cost of the seed, fertilizer, labor, fuel, and capital used by the producer. Also included are the eventual effect the fertilizer has on the water supply, the effect of tilling on soil erosion, and any other detrimental neighborhood effects on the environment that occur when corn is grown. These are usually long-term costs that add up without public awareness of the damage. Many are not borne by the producer, who brings the corn to the marketplace at a lower price than its true cost. Consumers buy more of the product than they would if the price reflected the higher true cost. Thus the market fails to generate the information required for the best resource allocation. In fact, it is ludicrous to expect producers to seek these long-term hidden costs and pay the expenses needed to prevent the problem if public ignorance is present. Consequently, public action is necessary to protect the ecological interests of future generations.

If these costs were trivial, as many with a strong pro-growth ethic argue, resulting market misallocation would be small. Unfortunately, there are increasing signs that accumulated damage to the planet may threaten long-term survival for all species, including human life. It is likely that resource exhaustion and the risk of nuclear war will pale as survival issues—in comparison to the battle humanity faces against toxic wastes in air, water, and land. Because these problems are not easy for markets to solve, there will be increasing interest in having collective action slow the process of degradation. Therefore, it seems prudent to increase rather than decrease efforts directed toward environmental protection.[1]

Information Costs

Incorporating neighborhood effects is not the only difficulty markets have in resource allocation. The costs of acquiring the information needed to make markets work can create difficulties as well. First, consider a market with low information costs.

Picture yourself at a market for a pencil. You examine all the pencils for sale before choosing, but you cannot be sure that the lead is strong or know if the eraser is smudgy. You simply buy one and take your chances. If the lead breaks easily, you will never buy that brand again. Chances are the maker will be out of business soon, because others will do the same as you. The cost of that information is the inconvenience of a poor pencil for a few days. Because the cost is so low, it is unlikely that anyone will set up a professional pencil-testing company and sell information on pencils. If such a firm starts, its customers will be able to share the information with friends without giving up the information themselves. That firm will fail since so many will receive its service for free.

If no pencil-testing firm exists, should the government regulate pencil producers and force them to use nonsmudgy erasers and strong lead? Regulators could inspect every pencil to ensure that you would have a better chance of avoiding a bad pencil. The criterion is whether the risk of getting a bad pencil is less bothersome than the taxes for the regulator's salary and the hassles of having regulators poking around pencil factories. Probably no one would prefer the regulator, especially if other pencil producers observed the fate of the bad producer and decided, for their own survival, to make only good pencils. In other words, for pencils, the information costs of government regulation are greater than the information costs of the market's self-regulation.

But suppose you need a person to remove your appendix. The cost of identifying bad doctors is much higher than that of identifying bad pencils. Although many people would be willing to pay a firm to evaluate doctors, the resulting information could be jointly consumed so that the firm might not be profitable. Also, if people must die for bad doctors to be put out of business, the cost of regulating appears less objectionable. Thus, society usually requires doctors to be licensed.

Between these extremes are lawyers, mechanics, and barbers, who are regulated in some way. Whether they *should* be regulated depends on society's comparison of the costs of information generated by regulators, with the costs of letting either market results or private vendors provide the information.

An alternative might be to require the producer of a good or service to be totally responsible for any damage done by the output. Fearing liability claims, doctors will not perform work without proper expertise, and airlines will carefully train and regulate their own pilots. They probably will do a better job than a regulator because they know their business better than anyone else.

The danger of strict product liability rules, however, is that they inhibit doctors and other producers of goods and services from implementing creative ideas. As a consequence, desirable innovation is retarded.

Regulating Natural Monopolies

Another area of market intervention discussed here is regulation of natural monopolies. If a product cannot readily be offered by two or more producers at the same time in the same market, we must choose between having a publicly owned company, a regulated monopoly, or a private monopoly company with power to set prices as it chooses. In the markets for water, electricity, natural gas, and sewage disposal, it is hard to imagine competing companies running lines through your lawn. Because of the lack of feasible competition, it is customary to have only one supplier but to rely on government to regulate prices at the level of normal cost plus a reasonable profit. An alternative to government-run or regulated natural monopolies is exclusive contracting. In this arrangement, a local government will list the specifications for a service like garbage removal and then entertain offers from competing refuse companies for the contract. The low bidder gets the job of being the only trash company for the community. In this way a natural monopoly-type product can be provided by the private sector, but competitive bidding still prevents monopoly pricing. This can work if multiple bidders are readily available.

Redistribution of Income

The last function of government to be discussed here, and perhaps the most controversial, is income redistribution. The first fact to keep in mind is that government affects income distribution in some way every time it acts, no matter what the issue. Every taxing and spending action redistributes income, as does every regulation or rule of the game. The question is not whether government should redistribute income, but how, how much, and whether and to what extent the effects are predictable.

This discussion will focus on issues that relate to direct, premeditated efforts to help low-income people. Farm price supports, spending on projects that benefit various groups, and tax advantages for special interests–these all redistribute income. But such programs often are intended to do other things as well and usually are not designed specifically for the poor. On the other hand, Aid to Families with Dependent Children (AFDC), food stamps, and minimum-wage laws all are intended to help those with low income.

A vast literature is developing on the appropriate strategy for helping low-income people, and it is necessary to sketch out the range of issues being discussed. One extreme is the view that the best strategy is no financial help at all. Charles Murray, in *Losing Ground,* suggests a program that consists of "scrapping the entire federal welfare and income-support structure for working-aged persons, including AFDC, Medicaid, food stamps, unemployment insurance, workers' compensation, subsidized housing, disability insurance, and the rest."[2] Murray mistakenly mixes welfare and insurance programs when he includes both AFDC and unemployment compensation in his policy recommendations, but his intent is not to punish the poor. He simply believes that those programs have created a group of dependent people without dignity or hope of escape from poverty. He suggests further that adopting his recommendation "would leave the working-aged person with no recourse whatsoever except the job market, family members, friends, and public or private locally funded services."[3] The implication is that these alternatives will result in a better escape from poverty.

An alternative view suggests that public assistance has in fact helped poor people to escape from poverty and become productive. Studies at the Institute for Social Research in Michigan have resulted in ten volumes of research on income dynamics that are summarized in *Years of Poverty, Years of Plenty.*[4] According to one of the researchers, this study reveals "a picture of economic mobility and of generally benign welfare programs that differs dramatically from *Losing Ground.*"[5]

The person concerned about poverty is left with enough conflicting views that any worldview presently held can fit well with someone's interpretation of the data. Yet few who come in contact with poverty would support the austere measures suggested by Murray. Although this function of government is controversial, it is sufficient for us to recognize that government has some responsibility in addressing the problem of poverty. This is true because of the complex causes and social ramifications involved, and because we live in a humane society where people in trouble are a group concern for both pragmatic and moral reasons.

Practical Concerns

The pragmatic justification for income redistribution rests on the fact that people find it costly to live in a society that has no structured means of providing income transfers to the poor. In countries where beggars line the streets, many people would rather pay a tax than face the constant decisions of whom to support and how much to give.

It is admittedly difficult for a government to sort out the deserving poor from those who take advantage of the system, but it is nearly impossible for the individual to make those decisions without investing a great deal of time in the effort to help. The large numbers of families below the poverty line make it difficult for an individual to know where to begin in the income-support process. The cost of an individual search to find out who is needy becomes prohibitive.

The problem of neighborhood effects also enters if private charity is the sole means of helping the poor. If you give to the poor, I benefit from your generosity without paying because they no longer beg on my doorstep. Consequently, I wait for you to give, and you wait for me to give, and ultimately income redistribution comes only from those with the most sensitive conscience.

Because this kind of transfer does not seem fair under common-sense scrutiny, society agrees to a general taxation with a more centralized distribution system. For the most part, some waste is tolerated until ways of identifying and eliminating it are found. In short, it is doubtful that private charity can be an adequate and fair way of solving the dilemma of the poor in our society.

Moral Concerns

The moral problem of income redistribution at the government level has at least two dimensions. First, to require someone to be self-supporting implies that the means for self-support is present. For many, the best job they can find brings less income than will support a family at even a low standard of living.

A small exercise should prove this point. Assume your best job opportunity pays $5 per hour for a forty-hour week. Assume also that all government funds are cut off, and health care must be part of your budget or paid for by the employer. Next, work up a budget for yourself as a city dweller earning take-home pay of $600 per month. If you have limited education and skills for advancement, what kind of a living will you be able to afford? If you are willing to work hard but have no better job to help you improve your lot, then the demand of society for self-sufficiency becomes punitive, and the moral issue of requiring the improbable cannot be escaped.

The second dimension of moral concern enters when it is recognized that economic well-being is more a function of relative than of absolute income standing. Those in the middle- and upper-income classes set the standard for success in a culture, and that standard is constantly held before everyone by the communication channels in society. Falling below the standard is depressing for most, but having no hope of attaining a level even close to it brings despair and saps the incentive to keep trying. Stories of people who have gone from rags to riches only increase the despair, since they only make the standard seem appropriate. The miracle is that upward mobility occurs as much as it does, but the data show that upward mobility usually is not sufficient for the poor to do much better than move to income levels just above poverty standards.

The moral implications of this problem should be clear. Those who have been able to achieve the standard through various combinations of privilege, hard work, and inheritance have a responsibility to those unable to reach the minimal standard. This moral sense of fairness underlies much of the social policy of the last thirty years. Many who are successful downplay this moral responsibility because they feel that upward mobility for the poor should be possible with reasonable initiative. They favor an elimination of public aid. This strategy overlooks the fact that the road to success is becoming more and more technical and skill oriented. Without training there is little hope.

To summarize this point, a legitimate function of government should put in place policies that redistribute income in ways that bring dignity and meaning to life. Where efforts fail, new ones must be found, because private charity is not a viable systematic answer.

This entire chapter has attempted to illustrate how collective action is necessary in a free society. Government is not an enemy of the marketplace but a complementary part of the whole of society. It defines the rules of the system, it operates stabilization policy, it helps to correct market allocation difficulties when public goods and natural monopoly conditions exist, and it redistributes income in a manner that is practically and morally acceptable.

Government Imperfection and the Theory of Public Choice

So far in this chapter we have focused on market imperfections, suggesting that some collective action may improve the situation. It has been implied that collective action can be expected to do the job effectively at minimal cost. This may be far from the truth. In recent years those who question the ability of government to be effective have had a strong influence on economic thinking. An entire area of study called the theory of public choice has developed, and a Nobel prize in economics has been granted for work in this area.

A brief sketch of the theory of public choice might be helpful. First, it assumes that people in the public sector exercise the same self-interest that private citizens exhibit. The public interest is, at best, only a secondary concern for those employed by the government. Second, since policy makers in a democratic government are usually elected to their jobs, they must behave in a way that will ensure re-election. The interplay between elected officials and their constituency, by its very nature, caters to special-interest concerns rather than the general welfare of the population. An example will illustrate this problem, which sometimes is called rational voter ignorance.

Suppose you are part of a labor group that is being hurt by the import of shoes from Hong Kong. If you lose your job due to the imports, it may cost you $20,000 dollars. This is enormous motivation for you to pressure your representatives for import restrictions. You will be willing to donate to the election campaigns of those who vote to protect domestic shoes, and you will be inclined to argue your case publicly wherever possible. Those in your situation may be few in number compared to the population at large, but you are well organized, highly motivated, and taught to use the political process.

Opposite you are consumers who will have to pay more for their shoes if tariffs pass. Perhaps shoes will go up fifty cents per pair. Even if the consumers knew the true cost of the tariff per pair of shoes, they would think it worth little to fight the legislation. In fact, any who had to spend more than fifty cents would think it not worth the effort. Since the cost of writing and sending a letter is more than fifty cents, elected representatives rarely hear from shoe purchasers. Thus, even if the total cost to consumers far outweighs the incomes saved for shoemakers, the tariff likely will be passed.

This is an example of inefficient government action, and it explains why the inefficiency occurs. Multiply this case by the nearly infinite number of concerns of various groups across the country. Add the fact that legislators might vote for each other's projects in order to gain support for their own. Then the magnitude of government misallocation of resources can be appreciated. Groups of all kinds take advantage of this flaw in democratic government. Consumer advocates, professional associations, seniors' organizations, and producer leagues are only a few examples of the lobbyist presence in government.

Other problems also exist when government acts. First, taxes often are unrelated to specific benefits, so that additional projects or favors seem to cost less than they really do. Second, people best trained to regulate an activity or industry are usually those who were trained in the industry and will eventually return to it. Therefore it is in their interest to have the government interfere as little as possible rather than to protect the public interest if regulation is needed. Third, federal budgets need not be balanced from year to year, meaning the costs of government are diffused in ways hard to identify.

Fourth, in stabilization policy, effects may be other than intended because of people's responses to specific policies. For example, suppose the population expects an effort to expand the economy through increased money supply. In this case, prices will likely rise rapidly as people protect themselves from the coming inflation by accelerating their buying. An illustration of this could be an auction where people believe prices are going to increase soon. Hoping to beat the price increases, they all bid quickly, causing prices to rise faster than they otherwise might.

Public-choice theory has its more complicated side, with various voting models and behavioral assumptions, but its message is that government, just like markets, has imperfections. When a market is inadequate, we are forced to choose between two inefficient alternatives: living with market failure or accepting government solutions. The choice an individual prefers often depends on one's philosophical perspective, and on how one perceives the costs and benefits of the choice. There is no bureaucratic god with perfect data and a completely unbiased perspective.

The Christian and Government Intervention

Little has been said in this chapter about a Christian view of government activity in the economy. In fact, believers have taken several approaches. First, there is what might be called the *strict constructionist* view. This view holds that the Bible is a guidebook for policy, and therefore government should not be involved in any activity unless a specific teaching is given in Scripture regarding a particular role of government. Typically, this position sees a limited role for government, even to the point of limiting tax collections to 10 percent of income because of the tithing principle.

A second view regards the teaching in Romans 13:4 as endorsing government policies that might be construed as for the good of the people. This provides a great deal of opportunity for the government as "God's servant" to engage in activities that relate to the four functions described in this chapter. Government, in this view, is not an evil force to be feared and distrusted but a friend of the law-abiding citizen. Since this view was taught by the apostle Paul under Roman rule, it is argued that the same ideas today would be even more applicable.

A third view attempts to balance the second view with the teaching in Matthew 4, which says that Jesus was tempted by the devil, who claimed to have control over the political powers of the world. This view recognizes the need for government policy to relate to the four functions discussed earlier, but it also is aware of the dangers of power and the tendency for corruption inherent in government (see Rev. 13). The functions most dangerous and difficult to control relate to the military and national security, where civilian control and public disclosure are the most difficult to achieve. This recognition that Satan actively seeks power in the world is consistent with the two-kingdom view of the world described earlier in this book. Government is a necessary and potentially good institution for the organization of the secular world, but ultimately it does not have final authority over the believer, who first of all is a citizen in the kingdom of God. In short, according to this view, government does have an important function to play in society, but it must constantly be challenged to do good and not evil to those over whom it exerts authority.

Discussion Questions

1. Why do conservative Christians often support more government in the military area and less in the social area, while liberal Christians often do the reverse?
2. Your answer to question 1 will likely be different depending upon which group you are more closely identified with. What does this say about right and wrong in the area of government involvement?
3. Is the critique of private charity accurate in your mind? What do you believe is the motivation for people to give to charity?
4. Luke 4:6 and Romans 13:4 give opposite views of the source of government authority. Can you reconcile these views by referring to material from this chapter?
5. What are some examples of partially public and partially private goods other than those given in the text? Try to rank them according to their "public-ness."
6. In what ways do you plan for the future? Are you as careful about the environment as you are about your retirement fund?

11

The Social Glue
of Capitalism

By now it should be clear that capitalism is a complex system
that can thrive when the social institutions are supportive and
the moral prerequisites are in place. However, the beauty of market efficiency in the abstract models must be viewed against real-
world applications of the system to see just how workable the theory is. Many countries around the world are moving toward free
markets with varying degrees of success. Hong Kong, Taiwan,
Singapore, South Korea, Chile, and China are a few examples of
rapid growth occurring along with increased private property,
freedom of exchange, and limited government in economic affairs.
Meanwhile, many long-time capitalist economies are experiencing
slowing growth, increasing difficulty creating good jobs, increasing crime, deteriorating cities, and a general perception that all is
not well. A third group, like the former Soviet Union and Eastern
Europe, are struggling to make markets work, with no guarantee
of success.

What accounts for the varying degrees of success and promise? To answer this question, I will reflect on a concept I would
like to call social glue. The case material will be that of Russia
and the USA. I have been involved with the Soviet Union and
Russia in various ways since 1983. Most recently, I worked with
a team of Russian and American faculty to develop a graduate
business curriculum for use in several universities in Russia. The

difficulties and challenges of these experiences have convinced me that economists need to pay much closer attention to the social and cultural fabric of a system than they often do.

The Western Social Order

It will be helpful to explore first the social glue of capitalism and then contrast that with the social glue of Russia's system. This contrast should illustrate how complex and precarious an economic system can be, and what is necessary to alter a system from its historical patterns. The contrast will also be helpful in chapter 13 when we assess the prospects for Christian infiltration of secular economic structures.

Figure 11.1 represents the key structures of a Western capitalist society like the USA, and figure 11.2 depicts a Russian-type society. The fabric of society is woven from at least five threads. Each one complements the others to create a social order. Each system is supported by an overarching ideological commitment that is consistent with all five of the component parts. When all five threads complement each other and are consistent with the overarching philosophy, a society will have a cohesion that allows it to proceed with purpose. A natural social harmony will be present. Policy proposals will pass and be accepted by the people. A consensus will be present on most important issues, and laws will generally be obeyed. Lawlessness is limited and effectively contained. Citizens will have a common understanding of what is fair and right. Figure 11.1, on the next page, shows the five threads of a pluralistic Enlightenment social order.

We have already looked extensively at how freedom in the *market economy* is thought to bring optimal production and allocation of resources. We have explored how it contributes to social harmony through a system of checks and balances called competition.

Likewise, *democratic politics*, with its grassroots representative structure and its majority rule, provides freedom and allows room for the dissenter to compete with alternative views. As in the

Figure 11.1
Social Order of USA

Pluralism

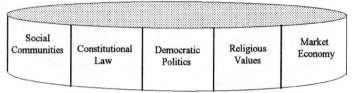

| Social Communities | Constitutional Law | Democratic Politics | Religious Values | Market Economy |

case of market activity where no one consumer's preferences are said to be better than another's, no political policy ideas are banned from discussion. The determining factor in policy is which idea sells the best.

Constitutional law is based on common law, precedent, and a separated judicial and legislative system. It gives order to social interactions. The rules of the game are specified and enforced so that the game can be played. Without this clarity, the freedom exercised in the other areas of the social order would be less meaningful. The law will reflect the ideology and values of the culture around it. It does not create and sell new values as an arbiter of truth.

Social communities in these Western societies are formed by the voluntary movement of people choosing to associate in neighborhoods compatible with their preferences. Citizens are free to move at will. They pick communities whose values are similar to their own. They find a community that balances tax and service trade-offs in ways that meet their needs. As in all areas of this social order, voluntarism is central to the formation of communities.

Finally, there must be some internalized *shared value system* that causes people to comply with the laws and expectations of the society. People must have some inner rudder that guides the definition of right and wrong. Since religious teaching is often the source of such a value system, this component of pluralistic social glue is precarious. Toleration has not been one of the strong features of religious history. Yet foisting one's view of absolute truth on others violates the voluntarism of pluralism. On the other hand, if an overwhelming portion of a population shares similar religious values, then these values can become an excellent contributor to social solidarity. The Judeo-Christian religious tradition was dominant in the population of the USA for much of its history. This made it possible for pluralism and religious intolerance to coexist. The result was a free, open, pluralistic society in politics, economics, and law, with a shared value system bounded by Judeo-Christian teaching. This provided a strong social glue that allowed the USA and other Western countries to develop and grow rapidly.

More recently, religious viewpoints have fragmented as new religions, secularization, and increased diversity within the Judeo-Christian tradition begin to surface. Homosexuality, abortion, and prayer in public schools are just the most prominent of a wide range of issues that are beginning to test whether a truly pluralistic social glue can exist.

In summary, the five components shown in Figure 11.1 come as a package supported by the *pluralistic* notion that any one view cannot be considered absolute or necessarily superior to another view. Apart from this favorable climate, Western market capitalism would likely have failed. For more than two hundred years, with this climate, the Western social order has muddled through various crises and has produced more economic goods than any competing system. Unfortunately, the past is no guarantee of the future.

The Authoritarian Social Order

For most of this century, the Soviet Union system, depicted in figure 11.2, was the main system competing with capitalism. The social glue of an authoritarian system of uniformity is much less complex than a pluralistic system. Those in power make the rules, and everyone falls in line or leaves, one way or another. Those who comply have basic needs met but are told how, where, and why to live. Values, laws, resource allocation, and political outcomes are imposed by the rulers. In the Soviet Union, the rulers were the Communists, and the principles of uniformity came from a Marxist-Leninist ideology. Now that entire structure has collapsed. Each of the five social components is now in shambles. When the economy was incapable of providing the goods, the authoritarian political structures lost their legitimacy. The alternative of markets, toward which these countries are moving, is a complicated social and economic process which is called transition economics.

Figure 11.2
Social Order of Russia and the Soviet Union

Uniformity

Functional Social Groups	Law by the Party	Authoritarian Politics	Czarist and Communist Values	Planned Economy

Rebuilding is an overwhelming task, even for the most optimistic. Since the law and the values of society came from the deposed authorities, the door was open for chaos. Formal law and order seemed to disappear, and organized crime moved in to fill the vacuum. Everyone began searching for values of any kind, and the economy degenerated into a chaotic, undirected do-it-yourself effort. Political freedom came almost by default and lost its luster when none of the other threads of the social order changed in an orderly fashion. Westerners, all too often, thought that a quick injection of market economics would transform this Soviet social order into a Western-style country. Quick privatization, instant monetary reform, open markets, and a strong infusion of capital were touted as the cure for socioeconomic life. Unfortunately, this society had been conditioned by centuries of feudal and authoritarian rule capped off by seventy years of brutal Communism. Almost nothing of the social fabric of capitalism existed, and the social glue of pluralism was a foreign notion at best. In addition, Russians were wary of what the Western capitalist package contained.

As piecemeal doses of capitalism were tried, Russians saw quickly what capitalism was like without its supporting structures: opportunistic entrepreneurs, a high lifestyle for those who made a quick profit, high unemployment as inefficient factories closed, runaway inflation, and unending crime. They saw that internalization of values had to be the primary deterrent from antisocial behavior, or else a police state would again be needed to enforce the law.

When we arrived to discuss curriculum, they insisted that our master's of business administration curriculum be values-based. Yet it was not clear what values they wanted or how those values would be grounded in a belief system. The challenge quickly turned from imparting technical economic solutions to instilling meaningful values in a culture. Slowly my focus moved away from being an economic consultant seeking to develop a generic values-based curriculum for a secular education system. Instead, I saw myself as a Christian, who happens to be an economist, seeking to tell my story of faith in hopes that people would see how my faith and economics interact. Multiple approaches were needed, but neither the infiltration model nor the modeling approach could be discarded. I felt compelled to support both the idea of a Christian college in Russia and our project in the secular universities. My Anabaptist moorings seemed relevant in both efforts as long as my values came through clearly in my work with the Russian economists. It was important that there were twelve Christians to act as a community of faith in the venture.

In summary, it is clear that transforming a social order from one based on uniformity to one based on pluralism is no small task. If the components are not present to support the pillars of capitalism, it will take a long time to make the transition. There will be no guarantee of success, since the forces of authoritarian uniformity are always present. Ironically, these forces seem almost desirable to those particularly hurt by the chaos of transition. What does seem clear to the Christian is that the authoritarian social order is not consistent with the values of the kingdom of God. Accordingly, the Christian constantly leans against that social order simply by practicing a genuine Christian faith.

But what of the pluralistic democratic world order. Can the Christian embrace it with enthusiasm and try to introduce it to an economy that has collapsed? Is it God's idea of an ideal social order? Here the answer must be no. To be sure, there is much in the system that can be appreciated, but as a unit, it is no substitute for the values of the kingdom of God, to which believers hold primary allegiance. The first problem stems from the conflict between a faith that claims that Jesus is Lord over all, and a social philosophy which holds that any viewpoint is valid that is not socially harmful. In this environment, the message that Christianity is the only way to God becomes offensive to many, and so the practice of an exclusive faith is discouraged. One example of this trend can be seen in the way Christian teaching is forbidden or discouraged in U.S. public schools. Yet public officials, under pluralism, have no choice but to exclude the practice of any one religion in public institutions. By contrast, in Russia I was asked to make sure that my particular values were represented throughout the curriculum which I was developing. Obviously, they have not grasped the full meaning of pluralism. Pluralism and Christianity are clearly not complementary views. They cannot coexist forever.

Second, democracy requires one to accept the will of the majority when only one path can be chosen. Since Christians cannot subject their consciences to the will of a society that is not Christian, they will need to reserve the right to exercise civil disobedience if necessary to practice faith. As culture moves into a post-Christian era, religious values will play a diminished role in society. Increasingly, rights supersede responsibilities in public discussion, and human interaction is governed by litigation rather than relationships. As this process continues, rights extend into entitlements of all kinds, and entitlements reduce the flexibility of the economy. Behavior is constrained by external forces rather than internalized values. Slowly the social fabric begins to fray, and decay follows.

The important question here is whether a pluralistic society is inherently doomed in the long run, or whether this decay could be reversed by a more concerted Christian infiltration effort. In chapter 12 the case will be presented that the utilitarian maximizing mode of operation inherent in Western pluralistic culture is inconsistent with the servanthood teaching of the gospel. This teaching will never become the foundation of any secular pluralistic system. Accordingly, believers will always feel like pilgrims and strangers in a foreign land no matter how benign the existing social system may be. This does not mean that Christians become separatists or isolationists in their culture. It does mean that they must learn how to lean against the grain of culture, how to critique market weaknesses, and how to stand with those who suffer. Chapter 13 speaks a bit more about these tasks.

So far, three things have been addressed in this book. First, the essential elements of any economic system were described. Second, a biblical model of economic relationships and practices was suggested. Third, the market capitalism system of resource allocation was explored, with a special emphasis on its philosophical moorings and sociocultural context. What needs to be done now is to deal with the most perplexing question. If, by Christian standards, all secular systems are seriously flawed, how can the Christian function in the secular world? The next chapter will take up that question at the motivational level by qualifying the pursuit of self-interest, the norm of the culture. Chapter 13 will approach that question by suggesting some intentional strategies that will help the believer keep the delicate balance between being in but not of the world. Chapter 14 will look ahead into the postmodern and post-Christian future to speculate on coming challenges.

Discussion Questions:

1. Try to paint a more optimistic picture of the future of the Western social order that will contrast with my suggestion of decay. What needs to change?
2. What is the vision of the Christian right for Western culture as portrayed by Pat Robertson, Jerry Falwell, and others? Can it work?
3. Speculate on whether one of the five ingredients of the social glue is dominant over the others? Can influencing one, change all the others? If Russia wants the Western package, will market reforms lead the way to successful transition?
4. What has been left out of this portrayal of market capitalism? Is the full story supported by these three pillars of capitalism: freedom symbolized by private property; social harmony from the pursuit of self-interest; and limited government, along with the sociocultural glue?

12

From Models to Reality: How Are Decisions Made?

At the Market Level
The discussion of markets has focused on some of the important concepts that make markets work. Clearly defined property rights, the pursuit of self-interest without power, and the limited but helping hand of government have been presented as important requirements for market capitalism to be successful. So too are the other social institutions that form the culture into a supporting framework for markets. Up to this point, the market environment has been presented as a simple auction setting, with bids and offers determining the prices that become the signals for resource flows. Such an image is obviously not the way a modern market system is structured. This chapter attempts to give a tiny peek into the way decisions are made by both consumers and producers so that the theory may be connected with what is observed in the economy every day.

Let us replace the simple auction image with a picture of a large number of wholesale and retail vendors who have stores or catalogs as outlets for goods and services. Each vendor has an inventory of goods that might last from a few days for perishable foods to several months for auto manufacturers. As a matter of convenience, prices are determined periodically and then held constant for a while. In some markets, like the labor market, prices do not decline easily, so layoffs rather than falling prices resolve surpluses in the short run. In general, prices respond much

159

more slowly to surpluses and shortages than an auction image would imply. Nevertheless, over time and through discounts, coupons, sales, quality changes, or rebates, prices fall when inventories climb above desired levels. Likewise, when sales exceed production and inventories shrink, prices rise through quality changes or hidden extra charges.

An area of economic theory called industrial organization studies the ways in which different market structures lead to different pricing strategies. Industries with only a few large producers do not experience price changes as quickly as industries like farming, where many producers exist. But even in international markets like oil, where large firms or cartels try to manipulate supply to gain a price advantage, prices ultimately will be governed by surpluses and shortages in the market. Thus the high price of oil in 1974, which resulted from a contrived shortage, led to an oil glut by the mid-1980s as new production and price-induced conservation took place. The turnabout took years, but market forces finally led to price changes, as the auction model predicted.

At the Individual Level: The Utilitarian Approach

The part of economic reality that must be considered next is the process by which producers and consumers make decisions in the market. These considerations are usually labeled *microeconomic analysis* because they deal with smaller components of the market rather than the larger, aggregate components of inflation, employment, and growth. According to the utilitarian approach, people make decisions using cost-benefit analysis or profit analysis. These labels immediately conjure up the concern that economists are basically number-oriented materialists with concern only for a cold, numerical bottom line, or monetary profit. Yet cost-benefit analysis is merely a structured way of explaining how most people function. When you decide when to get up in the morning or what sermon to preach or whether to walk on the sidewalk or grass, you are engaging in unconscious cost-benefit analysis and coming up with a bottom line.

To illustrate more clearly, take the situation of Bill, who has the option of walking on a sidewalk that is not the most direct route to his destination. Consciously or unconsciously, he has listed the costs and benefits of staying on the sidewalk. The benefits are that he saves the grass, people respect him more, and he has less chance of getting his shoes wet. But the costs are that he will not get to the destination as quickly, and he will lose the aesthetically pleasing sense of a stroll through the soft grass. This list of benefits and costs is not exhaustive, but it is sufficient for our purposes. The question is, What is his decision or bottom line?

Non-economists will argue vehemently that quantitative values cannot be put on the considerations mentioned. Some will even object to a priority ranking of the issues as if that somehow tries to make the intangible things of life coldly tangible. Economists, however, will insist that the mind is actually doing a careful calculation even if it is basically an unconscious process. In most cases, social pressure and a respect for nature and the beauty of grass outweigh the desire to arrive quickly at the destination. Therefore, Bill stays on the sidewalk. However, if his son has fallen off a skateboard on a sidewalk around the corner and appears to be hurt, Bill quickly revalues the calculations and ranks speed of arrival much higher and public pressure much lower. In fact, public pressure may now be a good in the good-bad analysis, and Bill takes the grassy shortcut.

Economists call the goods of any such calculations *benefits* and the bads, *costs*. Thus they label the process cost-benefit analysis. However, they do not limit costs to easily measurable concerns. That is why, for example, they are careful to include neighborhood effects like pollution in the full cost of producing a product, even though pollution costs can never be measured precisely. In many instances these costs must have some estimated value applied because there is no mind doing the work unconsciously. No supermind can unconsciously sense when a nuclear power plant is more costly than beneficial. Consequently, economists are called in to do the best cost-benefit analysis they can. Sometimes they assign the wrong values to some intangible bads, but their best effort is better than no effort at all.

Many of the issues that concern economists relate to the task of decision making in a business environment where specific numbers are generated from market prices. Businesspersons look at revenues from selling and costs of producing. They become the benefits and costs, and the difference between them is the *profit* or *bottom line*. This analysis is similar to the person on the sidewalk in that one has benefits, costs, and a bottom line. The reason some people criticize the businesspersons in this process is that most will not count the neighborhood effects of production (e.g., pollution) as costs unless society forces them to do so. However, individuals do much the same thing if they are more likely to walk on the grass when no one is around than when people might see them.

Thus, the most important ingredients of economic decision-making are these: first, understand the tangible and intangible nature of costs and benefits; second, discern which costs and benefits apply to a given decision. The first point has already been discussed, but little has been said about separating out the costs and benefits that apply to a specific decision. Using cost as an example, this problem boils down to determining which costs must be absorbed no matter what, and which relate only to the decision to be made. For example, *Consumer Reports* might say that it costs twenty-five cents per mile to drive your car. If you use that figure to decide whether to drive home rather than fly, you will be making a mistake. The figure includes insurance, license, and a bit of depreciation that will occur whether you drive or fly. Therefore, your added or marginal expense for driving may be only eighteen cents per mile, and your decision should be made using that figure.

In many affairs of life, knowing which costs and benefits are relevant to a given decision is complicated but, nevertheless, quite important. This kind of thinking applies to the decisions of the producer and consumer (microeconomics), and it also applies to the larger issues of national economic policy (macroeconomics). To think economically means to understand the costs and benefits of a situation, and to make decisions using only those costs and benefits that are relevant to a particular problem. This skill of relating only to the relevant costs rather than the total costs is called *marginal analysis*. It is not an easy matter to relate correctly to either total or marginal costs, but the better it is done, the better decision making will be.

Despite the bad press sometimes given to profit, it is the goal of everyone to maximize it. When you choose to take the car to work instead of walking, you do so because you believe your benefits exceed your costs. This profit is considered appropriate even though the road is now more congested for others, and there is one less parking space for another employee.

Profit plays one other function in life. If profits are particularly high in certain areas, they become a signal to others to join the same activity to share in the benefit. If a particular walking route is unusually convenient and saves substantial time, it will attract many walkers. However, eventually the grass will be worn off, the dirt will become more offensive, and the path will become so crowded that those who receive only a small profit from the path may find it just as desirable to stay on the walk. In the business world, profit serves the same function. High profits eventually attract other producers, who compete away some of the profits. Eventually, only the best producers remain, although the process may take a long time.

This utilitarian approach to resource allocation does not seem right to many Christians who feel it feeds on the self and excludes the servanthood calling of the believer. This obvious dilemma is faced in one of at least two different ways. First, some construct what economists would call a Christian utility function. What is profit for one person may not be profit for another. Although the method of dealing with costs and benefits may be the same with this Christian utility function, the values attached to the costs and benefits of many things will differ. Costs and benefits are not technical abstractions with explicit values agreed on by everyone. In fact, they are subjective evaluations of inputs and outcomes.

If the two terms are put into a ratio with benefits in the numerator and costs in the denominator, the result could be called a profit ratio or efficiency rating. Yet the value of numerator and denominator is always a subjective determination.
What one person calls a profit, another may call a loss. What is efficient for someone may be inefficient for another. An example of this difference occurred some time ago when an Amish farmer asserted that farming with horses was more efficient and profitable than farming with tractors and heavy machinery. The conversation between Mr. Yoder, the Amish farmer, and Mr. Furman, the modern farmer, is instructive:

Furman: How can your farming be more efficient than mine when you get ten bushels per man hour and I get one hundred?

Yoder: But I get more bushels per acre than you do, and I use no fossil fuel.

Furman: The fossil fuel is what makes me profitable. I use an eight-bottom plow, which means I can farm more land and produce more output and make more money than you do.

Yoder: You have more money, which you call profit, but I work all day with my family. I use natural fertilizer which protects the ground water and prevents erosion. I use no chemical pesticides either. I wouldn't trade my profit for yours.

Furman: Oh well, this may be a useless discussion because developers are interested in both of our farms. At the price they are paying, neither of us can keep farming.

Yoder: I have been offered far more for my land already than I could ever make in a lifetime of farming. But I have no intention of selling, any more than my father had before me. Farming is a way of life that money cannot replace.

The point of this discussion is not what the facts are, because the facts are meaningless apart from the values attached to them. Clearly, the farmers had different goals in life and therefore different definitions of profit, even though they were both profit maximizers. Each saw cost in a different way. If the cost-benefit ratio of farming is looked at from Mr. Yoder's point of view, his farm is more efficient. However, Mr. Furman has the more efficient farm from his set of values. Neither is right and neither is wrong from an economic point of view. Only the adoption of one value system over the other can resolve the issue--and then only in the minds of those who embrace that value system. Thus if the values are Christian, the profits will be appropriate, and efficiency will result.

This Christian utilitarian approach argues that decision making in economic life must be viewed in light of both accurate principles of economic thinking and a value system that is accepted as right. Terms like *profit maximizing, efficiency,* and *stewardship* are meaningless apart from value-laden presuppositions. They cannot be viewed as technical or absolute concepts. Because of this, it is not possible to evaluate capitalism as one clearly defined package. Instead, it is an explanation of how the world works under certain conditions. The method of thinking described in this chapter, combined with the material of chapters 8-12, make up the complex system called market capitalism. The difference between this system and the kingdom of God described earlier is that the two kingdoms have different values that underlie the maximizing method.

The glaring weakness of the Christian utility-function approach is that it simply defines maximizing behavior as whatever one chooses to do. If Mr. Yoder had gone berserk and burned all his crops, we could say that he was maximizing because his utility function must have put a high value on seeing crops burn. We could debate whether this is a Christian value or not, but there is little worth in a model that explains everything after the fact. Instead, we need models that assume behavior common to most people if we are to predict behavior with a high probability of success. In the world at large, it is not common to behave as a genuine servant to others, so perhaps the Christian utility-function model is not an appropriate way of understanding and predicting Christian economic behavior.

I know many people whose behavior I could predict best by knowing the needs of others around them and the teachings of Jesus rather than their own preferences. It would be wonderful if this servanthood attitude permeated our communities of faith to the point where another model for Christian behavior analysis was needed. To use the terms of modeling, if servanthood behavior was common to most in the church, then that behavior could be best understood and predicted by a model totally different in nature from the utility maximizing model discussed above. I am suggesting that a model which uses the preferences of Sam to predict the behavior of Al is more than an application of the utility maximizing model with uncommon values applied to it.

The Servanthood Behavioral Pattern

There is a significant literature about what is called nonmarket interactions. Jon Elster illustrates how social norms have power over behavior that is unrecognized in the utility maximizing model.[1] These norms are shared by other people, grip the mind and emotions, are not outcome oriented, and are not enforced from the outside. Although Elster does not include religious norms in this discussion, they would fit his analysis if they are behavioral norms that focus on practice rather than outcomes. According to Elster, these norms cannot be explained directly or indirectly by the rational-choice self-interest model of mainstream economics, yet they guide substantial portions of behavior.

Robert Frank uses the idea of cooperators and defectors to discuss similar concepts. Defectors will seek their own advantage in situations where it is advantageous to do so, while cooperators will behave on principle because they want to be the kind of person that acts on principle.[2] For example, if you are in a restaurant far away from home and will never be there again, why would you tip a waitress? Utility maximizers or defectors would not tip, but cooperators will because they want to be the kind of person that looks beyond themselves. Not to tip would make them feel like less than they want to be. Like Elster, Frank is not relating his ideas to religious behavior. He is simply questioning the usefulness of the utility-maximizing model for a wide range of behavior. Although there is a personal benefit of social solidarity that cooperators get in Frank's analysis, their behavior would not be expected if one uses the normal utilitarian maximizing model.

One interesting feature of Frank's analysis is that two cooperators working together both benefit more from their serving behavior than would two defectors who maximize their self-interest in a joint project. In a religious parallel to this finding, a servant-oriented community of faith will inadvertently lead to more pleasure than would pleasure maximizing in the secular environment. If a defector and a cooperator are teamed together in Frank's analysis, the defector dominates to the cooperator's detriment. The application of this possibility is the subject of the next chapter, where the viability of being Christian in a secular world is entertained.

From the work of Elster, Frank, and others, we can see that emotions, beliefs, and social norms do drive behavior in ways that seem counterproductive to the standard cost-benefit models of the utilitarian theorists. Elizabeth Anderson also illustrates how interpersonal relationships have a nonmarket character to them. Gift giving, exchanges of goods between friends, and handshake agreements all seem ill suited to the impersonal way markets are designed to function.[3] It is a short step from this analysis to the claim that Christian commitment is at least as powerful as social norms, emotions, and nonmarket relationships. From this background one can argue that there is a distinctly Christian nonmarket servanthood posture.

This possibility was driven home to me one day on a Mennonite Disaster Service cleanup trip. I was on my hands and knees picking up debris from a tornado in a farmer's bean field. It was hot, I felt exhausted, and I didn't even know who the farmer was. All around me were people from my denomination doing the same thing. I was eager for the task to be done, yet I did not go home. Something inside said that this was right to do, no matter what my senses were telling me. Perhaps this would fit as one of Frank's emotions or one of Elster's social norms. The label could simply be "servanthood calling." This nebulous nudge, when multiplied across many believers, leads to behavior that doesn't fit the usual pattern. Utility maximizing simply does not fit what is going on here.

This presents an obvious question: Do Christians function in an economy by following spiritual nudges from their servanthood calling? Is that how we function in our businesses, communities, and homes? I suspect the answer is yes, more often than we realize. This is especially true when we are relating to each other in the manner described earlier in this book However, the spiritual nudges are less nebulous than a non-Christian might assume. In fact, the servanthood calling is described and illustrated throughout the Bible, preached to the faithful each Sunday, and reinforced daily by practicing the golden rule in life. It is bolstered by God's grace and hopefully internalized to become part of the believer. In short, a practicing Christian is not a utility maximizer in any meaningful sense of the word.

In earlier work I took the Christian utility-function approach as a model for analyzing Christian behavior. I now put forward the *servanthood calling* as a model for analyzing Christian behavior for three reasons. First, it reflects more of the spirit of how we should be functioning. Second, utility functions that are too broad and include all motivations predict nothing, so the alternative model is not that attractive. Third, I believe that the way believers should function does contrast significantly with the way the world functions, and I want to emphasize that difference. Perhaps servanthood models will only explain and predict the behavior of those Christians who believe their calling to follow Christ is radical and countercultural.

This servanthood-calling notion is more easily comprehended when applied to individual behavior, especially intra-Christian relationships. Its meaning is less clear in the activity of an impersonal market where survival is the goal and competition makes the goal hard to reach. Most of this book, thus far, has dealt with the intra-Christian relationships of believers. The next chapter explores ways in which a believer, functioning in the servanthood model, interacts with a system that assumes personal utility maximization.

Discussion Questions

1. Is the choice to become Christian a cost-benefit exercise for you? If so, how did you quantify the costs and benefits? If not, how did you choose for or against Christianity?
2. You have been standing in line outside the concert hall for two hours, and now the announcement comes that the singing group may be fogged out of your town all night. Should your decision to stay in line or to go home be related to the fact that you already have stood in line for two hours?
3. Give some examples of things that you might consider efficient but that someone else might not. What are reasons for the differences of opinion?
4. On what basis are friends and spouses chosen? In what sense can these relationships be regarded as cost-benefit analysis?
5. What portion of your behavior (such as tithing, helping a stranger,...) might fit the servanthood model?

13

Being in the World
But Not of It

Thus far the conclusions of this book have made this chapter difficult to write. The secular world functions according to its own utility-maximizing desires. Its capitalistic system is precariously balanced by a social glue that has generated an unprecedented amount of goods and services to many. However, its pluralistic commitments do not offer spiritual values to its people. In fact, the diversity that pluralism fosters makes it hard to develop a moral consensus that can guide behavior and policy formation. What is left is a hedonistic spirit that promises social harmony while it glorifies individualism and self-serving. When a ballplayer spurns the $6 million contract to accept $7 million elsewhere because "I need to look out for my future," everyone seems to understand his logic. If he generated $7 million in revenue but settled for less, the owner offering the lower amount would pocket the extra million. There is no forum in such a system to address the morality of behavior. There is no right or wrong. It is simply the way the world works.

The term *world* is used in this book to mean the secular social order with its egocentric worldview. The desire people have to be gods to themselves has driven this worldview since the garden of Eden. The world is capable of good if it pays-off for the individual, but genuine selflessness or an open surrender to God as King is foreign to its thinking.

170

Over against this picture stands the Christian with commitments to a totally different regime. The believer makes value judgments on everything and opposes the world's standards when they conflict with Christian values. The conflicts are not trivial. Being in the world but not of it, is no small task. There are three areas in the range of human behavior. Figure 13.1 illustrates these areas. In order to emphasize both the importance of discerning proper behavior and the ambiguity that is often part of that discerning process, there is a continuum and a defined set of behavioral areas to help conceptualize how we might relate to the ways of the world.

Figure 13.1
Christian Behavior in a Secular World

A	B	C
Christian behavior that seems foolish to the world	Behavior common to both groups	Behavior that is not consistent with Christianity

Servanthood (modelers)   (infiltrators)   Self-interest

Where there is overlap in the servanthood and self-interest areas, there is no real conflict for the believer. Much of the daily activity of life is of this nature. Eating a healthy diet is good from both the self-interest and servanthood value system. Area B in figure 1 represents this kind of behavior. Likewise, having a car would seem to be in the overlapping area B, but driving a Rolls Royce would seem to be in area C. Volunteering to tutor an innercity youth who needs help may well be in area A. The process of sorting out which areas are which has already been discussed. The Christian community of faith has a big responsibility in this area.

The continuum discussed in the introduction of this book is part of the conceptual scheme of this chapter as well. The modelers, on the left side of the continuum, emphasize areas of separation from or nonconformity with secular thought and practice. (area A above) The infiltrators, on the other extreme, seek to penetrate the social structures to reform them. This process would make area C as small as possible. One of the themes of this book is that secular pressures have convinced believers that there is very little uniquely Christian behavior. Without realizing what is happening, believers are tempted to sell out to the world and have nearly all behavior fit the B area, as shown in figure 13.2. We mildly critique the world around us when the behavior of area C becomes blatantly offensive. Also, we occasionally do things in area A that the world thinks are foolish. However, most of our lives are spent comfortably in area B, where we see our faith and the world as being perfectly compatible.

Figure 13.2
Selling Out to the World

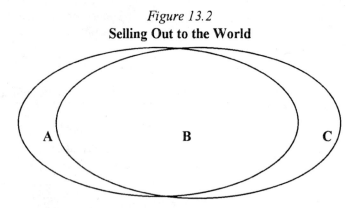

What follows are some suggestions designed to maintain the witness of area A while cultivating area B to the fullest.

A Doctrine of Nonconformity

The doctrine of Christian nonconformity with the evil of the world has nearly disappeared from the church's rhetoric and is increasingly absent from practice. Romans 12:1-2 makes it clear that apostle Paul saw a distinct difference between the spirit of the world and the Christian calling. Verse 2 states: "Do not be conformed to this world, but be transformed by the renewing of your minds, so that you may discern what is the will of God—what is good and acceptable and perfect." If we are conformed to the spirit of the world, it will not be possible to discern how God would have us use resources. Areas A, B, and C in figure 13.1 will be completely blurred. There is ample evidence that this is happening. We define and justify profit by using the world's definition of profit. Economic justice is defined more and more in market terms, and efficiency is defined by society's values. We have bought the structure of capitalism with all its powerful tools and fleshed out the structure with secular content rather than with the radical countercultural message of the gospel.

Both nonconformity and infiltration are relevant at various points in economic experience. Both seek to further the kingdom of God in economic life. However, the modelers are often misunderstood as uninterested in changing societal structures and unwilling to relate meaningfully to secular institutions. On the contrary, nonconformity itself can change people and social structures by presenting workable alternatives. Thus nonconformity to the world does not mean geographic or social isolation unless the secular environment is so hostile to Christian practice that persecution is inevitable. We should never give up trying to bend the world's values toward Christian values, and some of the most effective bending comes when society observes Christian values put into practice by people who believe those values can work. Increasing the area B in the figures above is an important part of the Christian calling, but it happens more as a by-product of explicitly Christian living than as a design carried out in the policy arenas.

This doctrine of nonconformity encourages Christians to hold a value system that results in decisions often foreign to the pattern expected or appreciated by society. In an open, pluralistic society, this fact may not be consequential, because people are willing to allow considerable deviation from the norm. But even in open societies, power and influence are acquired more easily by going with the crowd than by taking a countercultural stand.

The Beat of a Different Drummer

There are five areas where a Christian will likely walk to the beat of a different drummer than the one followed by the world. In these areas the believer should be nonconformed to the world and challenged to model a better way.

Restrained Consumption

First, Christians are called to practice nonconformity in consumption decisions. In chapter 6 this was discussed at length but needs to be reemphasized because most of the secular world recognizes no such restraint. The notion that some moral restraint applies to consumption and that the decision is not totally an individual one, is decidedly countercultural. To be nonconformed to the world in economic affairs means that consumption matters.

Ethical Standards

Second, Christians need to be in nonconformity to the world in standards of ethical behavior. Most people have ethical standards that involve compliance with the laws of the land or the regulations of a workplace. The norm is to be honest on tax returns, to fill out truthful time cards, and to pay off one's debts. For whatever reasons, most people, Christian or not, go by established rules that facilitate social and economic activity. Certainly the minimum standard for ethics is the best that the secular system can offer on an ethical issue.

However, Christian behavior requires more than compliance with secular norms. Christians have a higher standard of ethical behavior and a different method of defining appropriate behavior. Whereas the secular world often bases ethics on legal requirements, Christians look to the intentionality of the parties involved. If someone has inadequate or incomplete information, they should not be exploited because of their deficiency. Although they need not be provided free information, the cost of the information should be appropriate. The medieval notion of a just price has some components worth reviving because the situation of both parties in a transaction was to be considered by the Christian.

In addition to the ethics of transactions, there are issues of personal behavior. Here the full effects must be analyzed again. How are my health, my witness, my weaker brother or sister (see Rom. 14 and 1 Cor. 8), my community, and my family and children affected? Again, the framework is far more extensive than my own preferences. Thus one needs to consider the secular norms, the intentionality of the parties involved, and the full effects of the action.

Some examples of situations faced by Christians in everyday life illustrate these points:

1. I work for a company that transfers me to a division producing liquor, cigarettes, munitions, or a pure luxury good. Should I find another job?
2. I work for a company that buys another company producing one of the goods mentioned, but I do not need to work in that division. Should I change jobs?
3. As a personnel director, I must hire a minority person and turn down a more highly qualified person who is not of a minority group because the government mandates that action. Should I comply?
4. Some of my best workers have racist feelings and have told me they will quit if I hire the best applicant in the job pool, who happens to be black. Should I hire the black? Fire the racists? Delay until the black is hired elsewhere?
5. My company has 55 percent of the market share and is the price leader in the industry. Smaller companies are inclined to follow my price. Should I set a price that will maximize my profit even though it brings me a much higher-than-market

rate of return? Assume that market entry is impossible due to patent arrangements.

6. If the law allows me to pollute the air and add to the acid-rain problem, should I pollute to the limit the law allows to stay competitive?

7. As a worker, should I join a legal strike designed to get a wage increase higher than the productivity level?

8. As a worker, should I blow the whistle on another irresponsible employee?

9. As a consumer, should I buy a second home for recreation when others in my community are struggling to have one home because the best jobs they can find pay only fifteen thousand dollars per year?

10. As a producer, am I obligated to pay off debts legally wiped out due to my involuntary bankruptcy?

11. A friend owns a $300 computer monitor. It goes dead, and his repairman says it is not worth fixing. He offers it to you because you like to tinker with such things. A sixty-five cent fuse solves the problem, and the monitor works perfectly. Is the monitor yours?

This list could go on indefinitely because so many of life's situations are filled with ambiguities that make the practice of personal ethics a difficult matter. The objective here is not to solve specific questions but to point again to the primary group of believers that God has designed to help deal with these issues.

The community-of-faith focus of ethics is more than a matter of discerning appropriate behavior. When believers practice what they believe, the consequences can hurt. The non-Christian will not always be pleased with what a believer feels is right in a situation. The fellowship of believers must stand ready to share emotionally and materially in the hurts that result from radical discipleship. The less tolerant the secular world is of Christian values, the greater will be the need for this ministry of the church.

Stewardship of Creation

Third, Christians must be in nonconformity to the world in the use of creation. The problem of pollution externalities was discussed in chapter 10. Here the concern relates to difficulties that markets can have with allocation of costs over time. The market will bring about a rapid deterioration of the environment if people become shortsighted or pessimistic about the future. "Eat, drink, and be merry, for tomorrow we die" is an attitude that can easily prevail in an uncertain world. The closer society comes to this view, the more it pollutes and destroys resources that, under other circumstances, it would conserve for future generations. An implicit trust in science to bail society out of all kinds of harmful waste deposits would have the same effect.

The world does not appreciate creation as a gift of God, and it tends to view the present generation as more valuable than succeeding generations. Consequently, the world will more likely deplete the environment than maintain it. Although some may argue that this deterioration is not occurring, there is increasing evidence that problems are developing in the areas of water, air, and soil preservation. Thus, this third component of a doctrine of nonconformity involves a clear affirmation of God as Creator, Owner, and Sustainer of all resources and generations. This affirmation means that believers will resist efforts to allow the environment to deteriorate from one generation to the next. They may alter lifestyles that contribute to the destruction of creation or work for policy alternatives that will conserve rather than destroy.

Concern for the Disadvantaged

Fourth, believers will be in nonconformity to the world's standards in their attitude and practice toward the disadvantaged in society. This is true even though society helps those at the bottom of the socioeconomic ladder. Society has been willing to help the disadvantaged through aid of all kinds, and the commitment to this idea is strong enough that certain inefficiencies are accepted in the process. Handicapped parking spaces are accepted despite the fact that those spaces are often vacant long after the rest of the parking lot is full. Few object to this inefficiency, or most redefine efficiency in ways that allow for this assistance to the handicapped. However, it is one thing to provide assistance to the disadvantaged; it is another to identify with those people and share in their suffering.

Jesus identified with the lowly in special ways, and God chose to relate to the oppressed repeatedly at key points in history.[1] The biblical evidence on this issue should cause believers continually to examine the definition of success that they communicate to successive generations in the church. Terms like success, academic excellence, and social esteem are fleshed out in ways that often exclude rather than incorporate those who are disadvantaged and ill-equipped to compete in the marketplace. Those concepts, then, need to be restructured in our thinking to filter out components that foster attitudes of exclusiveness and elitism.

In short, society will provide impersonal assistance to keep hurting people at a subsistence level, but Christian people must also identify with their hurts and bring the healing that money cannot provide. The trade-offs made to do this will not be understood by the world; thus a biblically informed identification with the disadvantaged requires breaking out of the mold of the world.

Thinking Globally

Fifth, Christians are often out of step with their culture in that they think globally more than nationalistically. Thinking globally is a frightening venture because of the diverse cultures and philosophies that we encounter. The further we enlarge our perspective beyond ourselves, our home, our community, our country, and the Western world, the more competing ideas challenge our beliefs. For Christians, the task is particularly treacherous since we believe that the Christian way is intended for everyone. This notion can come across as extreme narrow-mindedness, particularly if it is coupled with the idea that the Western cultural, social, and economic way of life is superior to other ways.

Fortunately, it appears that the church has had enough experience in other cultures to recognize that the gospel can be both universal and particularized to a wide range of cultural forms. For many Christians, the same realization has not reached the economic areas of life. There still exists a deep-seated feeling that the road to a meaningful economic life is paved with Western views on individualism, materialism, markets, and economic growth which will finally result in a lifestyle like our own. Although some cultures may benefit from Western forms of social organization, it is usually counterproductive to assume that they must become like us.

Ironically, the move from a parochial view to a global view need not mean a radical rejection of markets or a move toward primitive living. It will require an effort to learn from and appreciate people with different worldviews. A person who thinks globally as a Christian will be forced to consider the enormous resource disparities that exist between believers in countries like Haiti and Rwanda, and Christians in the West. The model developed in chapter 6 is only a starting point in resource use because it does not pursue the global implications that arise from it. The responsibility of Western Christians to other believers as well as nonbelievers worldwide requires another book that will not be easy to write.[2] At least, it seems apparent that a nationalistic orientation toward international relationships will detract from serious progress in this area. In recent years, all over the world, the resurgence of ethnic loyalty and nationalism has led to violence and division. As global citizens, believers will be out of step with secular trends that prioritize interests according to national goals. To think globally without a strong national bias is to be nonconformed to the world's pattern of behavior.

In summary, the five areas mentioned where nonconformity to the world should be practiced include:

1. Consumption standards informed by values other than the world's view of the good life.
2. A commitment to ethical norms that goes far beyond the legal constraints of society, and a community-of-faith-based framework for discerning how those norms should be applied.
3. A clear theology of creation and resource ownership that protects creation from the egocentric behavior of any given generation.
4. Identification with disadvantaged people who are losers in the market activity of life.
5. Global thinking that seeks to overcome the divisiveness of nationalism.

The words of Romans 12:2, quoted earlier in this chapter, should ring more loudly than ever in our consciousness: "Do not be conformed to this world, but be transformed...." Immediately following this passage, Paul admonishes his readers to reject individualism and to blend their gifts into a community of faith. This message is relevant to Christians today who live in a society that considers individualism a key ingredient of social and economic organization.

Costs and Benefits of Nonconformity

Most of the ideas presented in this chapter must be fleshed out and practiced daily in ways that leave a clear witness to the values underlying the action. However, these ideas will not sell well to the non-Christian world that does not share Christian values or has a shortsighted approach to the future. For those who take them seriously, some of these ideas call for resource transfers toward the disadvantaged or increased costs of production. This does not imply that Christians are not able to function in the secular world. It does mean that they may not be as successful by the world's standards as their non-Christian counterparts.

Consider the following example. Mr. Cohen is a paper producer who does not hold to the values described in this chapter.

Mr. Franklin, on the other hand, tries to practice those values in his paper-producing business. Mr. Franklin has higher labor costs because he has given jobs to people who couldn't find work, and he pays them a living wage even though he could pay only minimum wage. He installs smokestack scrubbers to reduce emissions, even though the law allows far more pollution. He donates considerable computer paper to church organizations and several foreign-mission boards. Mr. Cohen does none of these things. Therefore, he has higher revenue and lower costs. Will Mr. Franklin go out of business? Perhaps, but if he counts the cleaner air in the community as a positive return, if he gains deep satisfaction from helping the less-employable people, and if his contributions to worthy causes bring joy to his life, then he may count it all a joy even though he has less money to live on than Mr. Cohen.

This simple story may be misleading at some points. Mr. Franklin may need to raise capital for his business in markets that insist on a monetary rate of return as high as Mr. Cohen's. Also, the higher costs of production may exceed the revenue brought in from the sale of paper. In this case, Mr. Franklin could not pay his suppliers, and he would lose his business. In general, competitive markets will not allow for much higher prices to support one firm's higher-than-average wage structure or antipollution equipment beyond what the law requires. Mr. Franklin cannot live on the intangible profits of satisfaction and joy. What should he do?

Several answers might be offered. First, Mr. Franklin's lifestyle will be more closely related to the expectations of his church fellowship than to Mr. Cohen's standards. This may provide some slack in the company budget that he could use for higher wages, more antipollution equipment, or paper donations. Second, his church body might wish to lobby the appropriate legislature to establish antipollution laws or property-rights arrangements that will keep the air healthy. If everyone must comply, there is no competitive disadvantage for Mr. Franklin, and the goal of clean air is reached. In the same way, public policy might provide assistance to the low-wage earner through job-related benefits that would eliminate Mr. Franklin's high payroll problem.

Third, a program of capital funding might be set up for investors who share Mr. Franklin's values. This may mean that a lower monetary rate of return is received, but the satisfaction of being faithful more than offsets the loss. As was mentioned in chapter 6, numerous investment funds exist that have restrictions for moral reasons. When this occurs, people are limiting their investment options, even if the monetary return is reduced.

It is not easy to be separate from the selfish mindset of the world and the harmful behavioral patterns that come from that mindset. Jesus recognized this when he taught his disciples to prepare for hardship because of him.

> If the world hates you, keep be aware that it hated me before it hated you. If you belonged to the world, the world would love you as its own. Because you do not belong to the world, but I have chosen you out of the world–therefore the world hates you. Remember the word that I said to you, 'Servants are not greater than their master.' If they persecuted me, they will persecute you; if they keep my word, they will keep yours also. But they will do all these things to you on account of my name, because they do not know him who sent me. (John 15:18-21)

It can be argued that if Jesus were here today, he would have a different view of the world because in the Western world, there is more toleration and respect of minority opinion than existed in his time. In one sense this is true, but in another sense the world is less religious and more deceptive than it ever was. Mr. Franklin may face a coercive choice: he must forget his desires to help the poor worker, the air-pollution problem, and the mission board–or go bankrupt. If he is alone in this dilemma, he probably will run his business like a secular entrepreneur, because the alternative of bankruptcy will bring even more suffering. Being squeezed into the world's mold is more subtle than most realize, and once one is in that mold, it is difficult to recognize what has happened.

The best defense against a sellout to the world is a community of faith that articulates a doctrine of nonconformity to the world and then encourages its members to be faithful even when the costs are high. In fact, as in the case of Mr. Yoder in the previous chapter and the apostle Paul in Philippians 3:7, what the world called *costs*, they called *benefits*.

Infiltrating the World for the Kingdom of God

If the proper base is secured, then the believer is prepared to enter the world as an agent for change in the structures of society. This goal of penetrating the world for Christ is the motivation for much of contemporary Christian higher education. Graduates who can climb the corporate ladder, teach in the best schools, get elected to key offices, or become the best lawyers are held up as models for the next generation to emulate. There is a belief that this effort will somehow change the social structures for good, or at least moderate the evil that might exist.

This model is not the same as the prophetic voice crying out against evil or injustice. It does not ask believers to openly rebuke social structures that lead to undesirable outcomes. Rather, it suggests that people permeate those structures and reform them through accepted channels of change. This is a noble undertaking, but it is not as easy as it might appear. Two separate concerns endanger the infiltration model.

1. The compromises required to permeate the institutions of society can easily lead to a sellout that means the message is gone by the time the position of influence is reached.
2. The message involves a conflict of worldviews that is difficult to boil down to the daily routine in which people work. It is easy to believe that no specific policy change can make a difference. Paradigm shifts cannot be reduced to any individual action.

The Temptation of Trade-Offs

The first of these concerns is easier to deal with. The world is full of trade-offs. When those trade-offs are considered bad, they are labeled compromises.

Perhaps the first thing that a new entrant into the infiltrating process realizes is that many people want influence and are willing to put in whatever time it takes to succeed. Thus, time becomes the first trade-off. Family, church, and social interaction get short shrift. Since there seems to be no alternative, the trade-off gets rationalized: "What really counts is the quality of time, not the quantity." At the professional level, the motivation to put in long hours is not money but desire for the advancement necessary to effect change. Thus there is little sense of guilt in the time trade-off at first—not until one looks back on years of workaholic activity does one start to question whether the trade-off was worth it.

The second trade-off comes when a policy or action requires some bending of an ethical standard. The question now becomes, "Is this where I take my stand? Should I wait until I am in a position to influence the decision more strongly?" It is easier to say nothing than to risk having your concern rejected with a loss of face and eventual influence. "Later, when I have power, I can make a difference."

A third process that dulls the initial fervor to be an agent for Christian change occurs when one realizes that no one is as big as the organization itself. Each person is in charge of a tiny piece of the action, and no one knows the overall scheme of activity. Everyone follows orders and feels little responsibility for anyone else's task. Labor relations, product liability, marketing tactics, customer service, and environmental impacts—these all are separate departments that no one person can understand. Therefore they cannot be critiqued as a whole or individually by anyone.

Slowly, the reform fervor disappears and the standard evaluation becomes the only mechanism comprehensive enough to coordinate enormously complex operations: *the market*. The great impersonal magic of relative prices answers questions that no individual can comprehend. Mr. Franklin's personal and interpersonal concerns are swept away by the harsh broom of competition. The fervor for reform was all a hoax, because no reform was needed—or so it seems.

Clearly this scenario does not apply to everyone. However, it is likely to be more relevant the more motivated one is to be an infiltrator for Christ in the structures of the world. It is hard to climb the ladder to power and influence and then critique the system that made it possible.

The second major difficulty of the infiltration model is that the message Christians bring to society's economic system involves changing ideas as well as behavior. It may be helpful to illustrate the difficulties Christians have with a secular economic growth view of how the world works by using a figure developed in part from ideas mentioned in Charles Kindleberger's text on economic development (see figure 13.3). Referring to research by Talcott Parsons and M. J. Levy, Kindleberger suggests that economic growth does not occur in just any environment. To be successful, it must be accompanied by changes in understanding and skills. Therefore, all five columns depicted in figure 13.3 move in the same upward direction at roughly the same time.

Figure 13.3
Worldview, Culture, and Economic Growth

1	2	3	4	5
Gross National Product	Understanding of How the World Works	Basis of Identity	Type of Interpersonal Relationships	Literacy
high ↑ ↑ low	mechanistic and rational ↑ ↑ providential or magical	what you do ↑ ↑ who you are	contractual and legal ↑ ↑ diffuse and trusting	high ↑ ↑ low

From a Christian point of view, the upward movement in columns 1 and 5 appears beneficial. But the same upward movement
in columns 2, 3, and 4 is less desirable and may be detrimental.
Surely a generalized higher standard of living, within reason, and
higher literacy rates are positive features of growth. However,
column 2 illustrates how growth and modernization move people
away from belief in Providence and toward rationalism and
mechanism. The Christian view of a transcendent Creator who
cares about the finite creation becomes increasingly foreign to the
modern growth-oriented world.

Column 3 shows how people see their identity more in terms
of what they do than of who they are. In biblical times, one was
identified by one's parent or family. Consequently, the family and
kinfolk were a much more significant component of one's identity
and a much stronger factor conditioning behavior than is now
true. Today one's name and family are less important than one's
occupation; a person who doesn't have a job feels a loss of
identity. Part of the difficulty many homemakers have is not only
the unexciting nature of housework but also the fact that in the
eyes of society, it does not count as work. Consequently, the
homemaker feels like a nobody in our modern world.

Column 4 illustrates the detachment that occurs between people as society becomes more complex. Instead of friendship and
trust acting as the glue holding social interaction together, society
now requires a contract, courts, and legal proceedings, and people
become obsessed with litigation and court rulings.

Taken together, these five categories represent a mixed picture. Economic development is certainly not free: some significant
components of meaningful existence are lost. Much of Scripture
was written in a time when the lower end of the continua prevailed, so much of its teaching promotes an awareness of the transcendent and a focus on meaningful family and community relationships. These teachings are not obsolete, because meaning in
life is still found in these relationships rather than in the increase
in GNP that has become the modern measure of well-being.

It is also important to note that the strongest pull toward ethical and moral behavior comes from belief in God, desire to honor the family name, and ability to trust in others and be held accountable by them. When these factors are weakened, the moral fabric of a civilization begins to deteriorate. Indeed, the price of economic development is higher than is often imagined. But it is impossible to turn the clock back on development. Technology and literacy have brought many good things that can never be undone, and never should be. Yet we need to restore the desirable qualities of the middle three categories of figure 13.3.

The Christian message now becomes clearer, but the agenda for infiltrators is hardly sharpened because the system that gave them positions of influence detracts from the values they want to promote. At best, an infiltrator can provide an example of personal integrity and a visible witness to what is really important in life. Only those who are called to faith will grasp the message, and they will understand more readily if they participate in a community of faith that models those values in authentic ways.

To summarize the discussion so far, the case against aggressive infiltration has been made on two grounds. First, personal integrity is often unconsciously compromised. Second, the very values that a Christian seeks to perpetuate are undermined by the process of development to which the infiltrator contributes.

A third caution against the infiltration process is that it leads to a revised Christianity more compatible with the secular world view. Daniel Bell, in The *Cultural Contradictions of Capitalism,* discusses how our American culture compartmentalizes areas of life and therefore can live for a time with contradicting values. Some of the contrasts in the political, technoeconomic, and cultural compartments of American life are indicated in figure 13.4.

The contradictions among the three areas of life are readily apparent. The group consciousness of political awareness conflicts with the individual and self-oriented focus of the technoeconomic and cultural spheres of life. The technoeconomic and cultural areas require considerable compartmentalizing of behav-

ior. According to Bell, no overarching framework can make sense
out of the confusion, and so the democratic capitalist era is in
jeopardy.[4]

Figure 13.4
Contradictions in Three Areas of American Life

Political	Technoeconomic	Cultural
Emphasizes group identity	Idealizes Individual initiative	Fulfillment of self in literature, drama and music
Idealizes equal rights for all	Self-maximization leading to public benefit	Relative standards of truth and beauty
Favors democratic collective action	Thrift and austerity leading to high productivity	No vision of the transcendent
Honors public virtue and self-sacrifice	Winnings are rewards, losses are punishments	Pleasure and leisure are goals

This thinking can be extended to the area of religion. Living
with compartmentalization and contradiction is not easy for the
Christian who sees in Scripture the need for consistency, even if
alienation and hardship result. However, the subtle desire to re-
vise religion to fit the mold of society at convenient points is one
of the devil's favorite ploys. The ardent infiltrator is particularly
susceptible to this temptation. Figure 13.5 illustrates the process
by which Christianity becomes revised so it can fit better the infiltrator's agenda. This look at how society can influence Christianity illustrates another risk of the infiltrator strategy and suggests a caution.

Thus the case for infiltration in economic life must be qualified by three concerns: first, risk to personal priorities; second, the
way in which economic growth affects social values of accountability and identity; and third, the way in which the values of the
world are likely to influence Christian thinking. Indeed, the risks
of infiltration are substantial.

Nevertheless, all of this is not a watertight case against infiltration, but rather a challenge to faithfulness in that effort. Believers need carefully to consider the compromises made and the values traded away in the desire to reform the structures of society. It is possible that a more radical countercultural expression of modeling might be more effective in the long run.

Figure 13.5
Societal Influence on Christianity

Christianity	Compromised Christianity	Reason for Revision
The body-of-believers concept of accountability	The individualized-faith notion of personal accountability	Influenced by the technoeconomic and 18th-century liberal political philosophy
The suffering-servant way of the cross	Easy grace for salvation	Influenced by cultural expectations
"You shall have no other idols before me"	Have the idols, but do not worship them	Influenced by technoeconomic and cultural values
A mutual view of social responsibility and caring	A self-sufficiency view of social responsibility	Influenced by technoeconomic concepts
A moral, deontological approach to ethics and values	A relativistic approach to right and wrong	Influenced by the cultural area

In the church the modeler and the infiltrator come together and learn from each other. Infiltrators must realize that they can infiltrate no further than their Christian values, properly discerned, can take them. Modelers must realize that the dynamics of the community of faith do have appeal to many caught in the secularization of development, if the message can be communicated effectively in the secular culture. In one sense the two functions of Christian witness are complementary, and in another sense they compete. When either function is pushed to its extreme position, it competes with the other. For example, the modeler isolated from society will not infiltrate at all and may lose all opportunity to witness. Likewise, the infiltrator who sells out to the secular institutions will have no gospel message to preach. Somewhere between the two extremes lies an optimal mix for a given environment. It is the thesis of this book that the present mix in economic life for many Christians has swung too far toward the infiltrating extreme, to the neglect of faithfulness in discipleship and the building of the community of faith.

Discussion Questions

1. List some concrete ways in which you feel the tension between being a modeler or an infiltrator.
2. Work through some of the ten ethical dilemmas listed on pages 175 and 176. Add your own real-life dilemmas, and discuss how a Christian value system will call for a different response from a non-Christian value system.
3. Do you think it is important for theological reasons to be heavily involved in the environmental concerns of our day?
4. Why does God seem to be more involved with poor people at key points in history than with rich people (Luke 6:20; 1 Cor. 1:26-29; James 2:5-7)? Is there any significance in the fact that Jesus was born into a lowly situation, lived a simple life, and died with virtually no possessions (Luke 9:58)?
5. What obligation do Christians in developed countries have to believers in poor and developing countries of the world? Can the model of chapter 6 be applied globally in some manner?
6. Does Mr. Franklin have an obligation as a Christian to do more in his business than Mr. Cohen is doing in the areas of wages, benefits, and environmental protection?
7. Do you know Christians in significant places of power and influence who struggle with dangers from infiltrating the world for Christ? If so, invite them to share their feelings with you to see if the problems of infiltration discussed here are valid.
8. Is it necessary that the five trends in the growth model of figure 13.3 occur simultaneously? Could some be avoided?

14

What of the Future?

In chapter one, four worldviews were discussed. The postmodern view has not been specifically addressed so far in this book. It is only emerging in subtle ways and cannot be easily defined so early in its development. One can only speculate about what it means for Christians and for economics. The following quotation about some who are exploring intellectual change is helpful in setting the stage for some comments about what is coming in the decades ahead.

> At bottom, these observers see the breaking up of secular, rationalist humanism, a philosophy that germinated during the Renaissance, reached full flower in the 18th-century Enlightenment, and still permeates Western culture today. Progress is the promise of humanism; reason is its tool.
>
> Through reason, man would discover the "laws of nature." If man could just know enough and apply that knowledge, things would get better and better.
>
> But now doubts are eroding this secular faith. Nature, once viewed as inherently orderly, is coming to be viewed by many (although certainly not all) scientists as inherently disorderly. And human history once viewed as something that rational man could bend to his liking, is increasingly viewed as a force unto itself.[1]

This breakdown of the Enlightenment modern worldview has many implications for Christians interested in economic matters. At its core, the shift in thought is a movement from foundationalism, or a belief in discernible absolute truth, to a concept that absolute truth, if it exists, is unknowable. This post-modern view assumes that we can only perceive things from where we are. Our perception will be unique to us and therefore cannot be viewed as absolute in any way. David Lyons describes how such a move to relativity occurs. "Today's more general acceptance of the view that our observations depend on assumptions, and that those assumptions are connected with worldviews and with power positions makes relativity, not to say relativism, seem more natural."[2] Assumptions, worldviews, and power positions are not permenantly fixed or absolute over time, so an enduring objective reality or truth is elusive. We can only have perceptions that may be helpful for a particular curcumstance or occasion in history.

If truth is relative, then there can be no meaningful universal systems of the kind proposed in economic theory or the Christian faith. Any attempts to impose universal principles is a violation of another's right to an alternative viewpoint. "All knowledge, postmodernists claim, arises from finite, relative perspectives of particular knowers; thus all efforts to elaborate it into universal systems are efforts to invest one's perspective with inappropriate, coercive authority."[3] To be genuinely postmodern, one needs to reject all absolute truth claims.

Lacking universal systems around which to organize discourse, the postmodern talks of *chaos* and *hyperspace* in science.[4] In literature, the concept is *deconstructionism,* in which the reader interacts with the text to discern its meaning for the reader rather than the intent of the author. In theology, proponents of this viewpoint talk of *hermeneutics* or *contextualization,* words which, when used by the postmodern, can be thought of as similar to deconstructionism. The written word as an object of a writer, with meaning in itself, is now part of the old worldview in which objective truth could be grasped with proper scientific study. In short, since truth is not discernible, postmoderns must create their own understandings which can be only interpretations from one vantage point.

In order to prevent the moorings of the mind from becoming completely unglued, similar ideas are grouped into what is frequently referred to as traditions or communities. These traditions provide a framework for dealing with perceptions of reality. A religion could be an example of a tradition. Believers hold common views on a wide range of issues and label them as truth for them. To claim them as exclusive truth would be impossible in this new world of relativity. Accordingly, religion can play a vital role in life according to this scheme, but it cannot claim to have a grasp on any ultimate truth.

All of this is touted as a freeing escape from the oppression of imposed order. J. L. Burkholder, in writing about this shift in worldview, suggests that "a subtle and profound change has come upon us with respect to how we perceive reality. This change is sometimes celebrated as liberation. It is to be liberated from a world of external restraints in favor of subjective freedom."[5] Unlike the freedom of the modern world, which was bounded by the order of creation, this new freedom has nothing objective to give it boundaries.

In summary, the postmodern world is based on the notion that we cannot know ultimate truth. It holds that knowledge is a subjective matter in which personal perspective, context, frame of reference, and individual interpretation are the keys to meaning. Therefore, we cannot systematize or generalize knowledge in any useful way.

Having examined briefly some themes of the coming worldview, it is important to consider where this thinking will take economics and Christianity. During the last fifty years, modernism has taken economic thinking on a roller-coaster ride of optimism, uncertainty, and now skepticism. The post-World War II era up until the early 1970s brought economic expansion and optimism. It seemed as though we had figured out how a market economy, properly tuned, could solve the core economic questions. My generation optimistically went into graduate school to learn the tools that would make the world economically sufficient at last.

But something went wrong in the 1970s. The oil embargo and the ongoing Vietnam War were the parts of the iceberg of trouble that showed most prominently above the water, but much more was happening below the surface. The social programs instituted in the 1960s showed signs of being counterproductive. Inflation and unemployment began to grow together as the expectations of people started to feed quickly back into behavior. A burst of technological change set the stage for the era of the techno-haves and the techno-have-nots. Out of this uncertainty came a call to return to our modernist roots. If we could only develop truly free markets, we would overcome the malaise that was upon us.

People will long debate whether or not the experience of the USA in the 1980s constituted a return to free markets. Many feel it was a feeble attempt that needs to be perfected now. Others feel it was a sufficient attempt to show us that such a strategy is not adequate for our problems. What seems to have lasted from the 1980s is a more unequal distribution of pretransfer income, structural deficits, and a skepticism about both markets and government as vehicles for economic success. The best we can do is look at countries, recovering from economic shambles with newly freed markets, and feel encouraged by their growth rates. That is small comfort when we see the low growth rates, collapsing infrastructure, high structural unemployment, and seemingly aimless economic policy of the matured capitalist countries.

The policy is aimless because there is no clear vision about what will work. The world of economics no longer seems to have a mechanistic order to it. The reader of popular literature could see the change coming. From *Future Shock* to *Megatrends*, to *Power Shift*, and now to *Paradox*, the message kept coming. The forces of change are overwhelming, and they do not fit the standard categories or models that we like to use to organize our thinking. Peter F. Drucker illustrates how the "knowledge society" has unglued the traditional communities and has left a void that demands a new social sector. "The right answer to the question Who takes care of the social challenges of the knowledge society? is neither the government nor the employing organization. The answer is a separate and new social order."[6] Drucker goes on to describe this new sector as a collection of private nonprofit volunteer social-service organizations. In postmodern terms one might call these organizations, communities of action. The problem is that this new social order has not yet come together effectively. Since such institutions tend to form in a spontaneous manner, this leaves the future of the new social order ambiguous. The politics of the 1990s has illustrated how difficult it is for government to fill in the gaps in the social order. Without some new social order, many see continued social fragmentation and chaos.

Mainstream economics has attempted to meet the challenges by being more vigorous in inductive and deductive theory building and policy formation. If the mechanistic market could be better understood and relied upon, we could be more efficient, produce more, and restore order in place of the disarray.

Politically, increasing numbers have climbed on the bandwagon that believes the problems are due to the liberal politics of the 1990s. They predict economic collapse unless a swing to the conservative right occurs. The 1994 November elections were evidence of this thinking at the grassroots level. In other words, for both economics and politics, the answers still lie in the modern Enlightenment worldview.

What is missing in this analysis is that the foundations of the modern worldview are crumbling. Pluralism has served as a powerful complement to individual freedom in modern thought. But pluralism, when fully internalized, leads to the belief that there are no uniquely true answers. There are only interest groups with their own answers. The paradox is that unbounded pluralism and objective truth do not live in the same house forever. They have coexisted now for two or three hundred years because pluralism was bounded by various social and religious constraints. But pluralism is now being true to its nature by evicting objective truth and setting up housekeeping alone. It is this logical progression of pluralistic thinking coupled with a relational rather than objective

view of reality that is at the heart of the postmodern social unglu-
ing presently under way.[7]

Unfortunately, the postmodern world has little to offer in
place of the modern world. Even Stephen Hawking, a scientist
who still hopes for a grand unifying theory of the universe, admits
that there will always be sufficient uncertainty to make the pre-
diction of events unlikely.[8] The orderly world has disappeared,
and economics is feeling the effects of that claim.

One way to describe the dilemma economics faces is to examine the questions that economics must now deal with. For several
centuries the primary question was, How can we best increase
material well-being in society? Increased production became the
foremost concern, and markets became the engine that delivered.
Tuning the engine and increasing its horsepower dominated the
economic agenda from the eighteenth to near the end of the twentieth century. The task was perfectly suited to the modern worldview, and the success of the effort has become apparent around
the world. In a general way, there is a perception that economics
can deliver the goods if given a favorable environment to do so.

But with that perception has come a growing awareness that,
for all the production, we have generated little meaning and purpose in life. The questions now become, What does all this activity mean for us? Are we now closer to the good life? Why do we
do what we do? Postmodernism springs from these questions because people cannot find answers to them in modern thinking. If
economics seeks to be relevant to the needs of people in the next
century, it must speak to the concerns of meaning.

Economists who view the problem in this way might paint a
scenario for the future of economics as follows: First, the mechanistic system-building efforts of economists will cease to dominate
the mainstream. Routine patterns of behavior assumed by rational-choice theory will be qualified by a wide range of interdisciplinary nonmarket variables.[9] As society becomes more hetero-
geneous, the ability of standard theory to predict effectively will
diminish. The "invisible hand" (see Adam Smith, chapter 9) will

become less dependable as a market guide. Economic theory will be viewed as contextual rather than universal, and values will become part of the discussion again. Resource allocation can only be worked out with the help of the visible hand of business, government, and something like the new social sector proposed by Drucker. The neat equilibrium models of neoclassical market theory will be replaced by disequilibrium models that focus on process. Behavior conditioned by group norms will do more to allocate resources than the actions of individual consumers operating in free markets.

In business, the case of the baseball industry illustrates the notion on the part of owners that their industry is a special case that free markets cannot solve. In a world where everyone's viewpoint must be respected, everyone can declare oneself a special case.[10] The burden of proof to claim otherwise will rest upon those who oppose the special-case treatment. In most cases, such a proof will have no guarantee of success.

Another mainstay belief of the Enlightenment was a notion that the machine of economics and technology would bring about constant progress over time. Now David Ehrenfeld writes that "the idea of progress is the disease of our time. In truth, we are not inventing our future. We are just engineering changes whose outcomes we cannot predict and which often turn out to be terrible."[11] In the past, these critiques of economic activity came from dissidents and the fringe crowd. Now the concerns seem to be spreading.

Irving Kristol, of the American Enterprise Institute, speaks of these times as a "shaking of the foundations of the modern world." He is one of those who claim that "we are at a unique moment in Western culture, the collapse of secular, rational humanism."[12] These claims seem more plausible when one observes how these ideas filter down unawares to everyone. Political correctness is one example of this thinking at work. No one has authority to critique the view of another, and no standard is superior to another. Beauty in art or music is in the eye of the beholder. No absolute criteria exist with which to compare creativity. In the legal realm, what appears like a frivolous case to some wins large settlements for others.

Enormous effort must go into protecting oneself from all sorts of potential claims because there is minimal consensus on what is right or wrong in interpersonal relationships. Definitions of discrimination, reverse discrimination, abuse, and irresponsibility are becoming subjective and confused. In natural science, plant life and animals may now have similar standing to human life. Freedom of choice takes precedence over the absolute right of a fetus to live. The postmodern world simply cannot tolerate universal norms in any area of life, and so a vacuum of values is becoming apparent.

But vacuums do not exist for long. Religions and pseudoreligions proliferate. Movements spring up everywhere. Buried in nearly every interest group, be it a street gang or an environmental lobby, is a need to explain how the world works and how to make sense out of its happenings. Kristol observes that people want more than scientific rationalism and material progress. "They want community and they want transcendence."[13]

We should not be surprised. For community and transcendence are precisely what the rational humanist world of modernity did *not* offer. For three centuries people were taught that individualism and the rational-material-scientific world were what mattered. Christians often led the way, extolling the modern world and its order and predictability. As noted in chapter 13, the gospel was frequently accommodated to fit the precepts of modernity. Occasional prophetic attacks on "secular rational humanism" were sufficient penance for worshiping regularly at the altar of the Enlightened world. Christians wanted rational humanism destroyed at the personal level, but they supported it at the systemic level. But who could blame the church? It had to escape from the medieval trappings of regimented communities, and it could not ignore the benefits of the modern world. It could be argued that the costs of accommodation have been high.

Since community and transcendence are deep needs of post-modern people, believers must look seriously at how Christianity speaks to these needs. Many groups are putting increased focus on worship. The majesty and glory of a transcendent God to be worshiped is attracting some from mainstream evangelical circles which emphasize a warm personal nontranscendent relationship with Jesus.

The growth of the small-group movement within large congregations is evidence of an effort to develop community among people. The need for this kind of intimacy as a complement to the majestic transcendence of God is one reason why this book has a strong community-of-faith emphasis.

Finally, although believers recognize that grasping absolute truth may be difficult in many areas of belief and practice, we still believe there is the truth of God manifest to us through the person of Jesus, the incarnate Son of God. This belief means more than personal salvation to those who hold it. It provides a context from which to do economics in both the modern and the postmodern world, because in Jesus, the Logos and wisdom of God, "all things hold together" (Col. 1:17). This New Testament concept of the Logos used by the apostle John in the first verse of his Gospel communicates a theme which is meaningful to economists seeking to understand how the world works. There is structure, there is order, and there is purpose in our world.

However, that order is not the purely mechanistic, value-free, God-absent structure of the Enlightenment world. Rather, it is an order that is God-directed and complements the teaching of Jesus. That order makes modern science possible, but it reaches fullest flower for the social sciences when it incorporates into the discussion the human need for transcendence and community. The rational-objective side of analysis cannot be separated from the subjective value-laden part of life.

Economists need the Logos of creation and the Logos made flesh to face the postmodern world that knows neither. The Logos of creation is the source of successful econometrics and system modeling. The Logos made flesh pushes the Christian analyst beyond the rational maximizing economic person to include the whole person. It pushes the Christian economist to become more interdisciplinary, more concerned with emotions, feelings, and aesthetics. It seeks to uncover the meaning of things as well as merely predicting outcomes. It explores values and becomes, once again, a branch of moral philosophy. This is not a job for the fainthearted, but it is a task that will speak to the postmodern mind in ways that contemporary mainstream economics can not. It is a task for which the Christian economist should be particularly well suited.

Discussion Questions

1. Debate the question about programmed prayer in the public schools. Would you vote for or against having public schools offer students a chance voluntarily to recite a prayer from one religion only? Why? Answer in terms of your view of pluralism.
2. Have we oversold science? How much confidence do you have in the claim that if scientific research is perfected, we can cure all human problems? Give a modern and a postmodern answer.
3. Do you see the instability and gridlock of the American political scene as just another problem of weak politicians or as a consequence of postmodernism pushing out modernism.
4. Why will the postmodern world make it impossible for economists to continue to be glorified technicians or mechanics?

Notes

Chapter 2: Allocation of Resources

1. Adam Smith (in the eighteenth century) argued that nonmaterial considerations can be as powerful as material ones, or even more powerful. Smith, in *The Theory of Moral Sentiments* (Indianapolis: Liberty Classics, 1976), presented justice, benevolence, and prudence as the three primary motivations of all human action. He analyzed the desire for honor, respect, advancement in society, wealth, and other motivations as subsets of those three primary motives. In the late nineteenth century and throughout the twentieth, thinkers identified as members of the Austrian School of Economics have emphasized the idea that incentive includes anything a person desires, whether material or nonmaterial, whether selfish or self-sacrificial. One representative of that school, Ludwig von Mises, develops these ideas in *Human Action: A Treatise on Economics,* 3d rev. ed. (Chicago: Regency, 1966). Evangelical philosopher Ronald Nash discusses this point extensively in *Poverty and Wealth: The Christian Debate over Capitalism* (Westchester, Ill.: Crossway, 1986), chap. 4, "The Theory of Subjective Economic Value." Such thinkers tend to see material rewards as only intermediate and desirable only to the extent that they are means to the fulfillment of persons' nonmaterial goals (happiness, charity toward others, learning).

All of this may be true, but these arguments serve to make capitalist behavior more justifiable rather than to refute the idea that capitalism allocates goods and services efficiently because material rewards are pursued as the key means to the good life. Common perceptions further support the view presented in this book, that profits are needed to drive the system and that lower taxes will increase the work effort. The fact that increased profits or take-home pay might be donated to the church does not alter the fact that the desire for material rewards drives the system. Whether profits are a primary goal or simply a means to charitable activity is irrelevant to the functioning of the system, even though they are important considerations in assessing its moral character. It is a bit ironic that some who argue the loudest against the notion that capitalism is driven by the desire for material gain often use the high level of material well-being of the capitalist societies as proof of the superiority of market capitalism. A system should be evaluated on how well it delivers on the goals it seeks to achieve. Few if any studies compare systems by look-ing at the values put forth by Smith, von Mises, and Nash.

2. Charles Handy, *The Age of Paradox* (Boston: Harvard Business School Press, 1994), 6.

3. Robert L. Heilbroner, *The Worldly Philosophers: The Lives, Times, and Ideas of the Great Economic Thinkers,* 5th ed. (New York: Simon and Schuster, 1980), 32-33.

4. Peter L. Berger, *The Capitalist Revolution: Fifty Propositions About Prosperity, Equality, and Liberty* (New York: Basic Books, 1986), 211.

Chapter 3: Biblical Background to Economic Thinking

1. Millard Lind, "The Economics of the Hebrews," an unpublished paper presented at the Regional Consultation on the Meaning and Importance of Money in Following Jesus, Sept. 1980, 1.

2. There is some question whether the Jubilee principle was specifically designed as a redistribution instrument or a limitation on irresponsible bor-rowing. If the land that was transferred to someone else for a time was merely collateral for a loan, and if the size of the loan was limited to the expected return from that land between the time of the transfer and the Jubilee year, then the return of the land is merely a return of the collateral after a loan is retired. E. Calvin Beisner presents this view in *Prosperity and Poverty: The Compassionate Use of Resources in a World of Scarcity* (Westchester, Ill.: Crossway, 1988), chapter 5. Beisner states that "the provisions of the Jubilee year were designed not to promote economic equality but to prevent one fam-ily member's destroying an entire family's means of productivity, not only in his own generation but also in generations to come, by selling, permanently, the family's means of production." This interesting interpretation, rather than arguing against a redistributive focus of the Jubilee, actually provides a more forceful case for God's interest in income redistribution. God programmed into the structure a mechanism that acted as a deterrent to destitution even across generations. By restricting the borrowing of one party, the Jubilee also re-stricted the lending ability of another party that had a differing view of present and future income. This prevents what otherwise may become larger income disparities over time. Effective income redistribution mechanisms need not be pure income transfers, although many think of them in those terms. A pre-ferred way of dealing with inequities is to build in structural safeguards against the poverty-causing process. Indeed, there is no way to divorce the Jubilee concept completely from redistribution considerations, but it is impor-tant to see it as part of the entire Hebrew social system that is discussed later in this chapter.

3. Meir Tamari, *With All Your Possessions: Jewish Ethics and Economic Activity* (New York: Free Press, 1987), 59.

4. Tamari, 28.

5. For a sociological study of the New Testament world, read Derek Tidball, *The Social Context of the New Testament: A Sociological Analysis* (Grand Rapids: Zondervan, 1984).

Chapter 4: The Two-Kingdom Approach to the Bible

1. Richard H. Hiers, "Kingdom of God," in *Harper's Bible Dictionary*, ed. by P.J. Achtemeier (San Francisco: Harper & Row, 1985), 527-29.

2. Ronald J. Sider, "The Christian College: Beachhead or Bulwark?" *The Other Side* 14 (Aug. 1978): 18-19.

3. D. A. Carson, "Matthew," in *The Expositor's Bible Commentary*, ed. Frank E. Gaebelein, 12 vols. (Grand Rapids: Zondervan, 1984), 8:373.

4. Carson, 374.

5. Howard A. Snyder, *The Community of the King* (Downers Grove: InterVarsity, 1977), 31.

Chapter 5: Reading the Bible With Modern Glasses

1. John W. Betlyon, "Coinage," in *Anchor Bible Dictionary*, ed. D. N. Freedman et al. (New York: Doubleday, 1992), 1:1076-1089, esp. 1083.

2. Robert L. Heilbroner, *The Nature and Logic of Capitalism* (New York: W. W. Norton, 1985), 34-35.

3. The term *productive capital* may be confusing to some. For those who are not familiar with the way economists use this concept, the term *productive machinery* would be a helpful substitute throughout this chapter. When a typewriter replaced a pencil, the production of the writer increased dramatically. Likewise, the computer has multiplied the output of the writer even more. The same process of output increase occurred when a shovel replaced hands and a backhoe replaced the shovel. Inert machinery has the same kind of power that a grain of wheat has, although that was not recognized until relatively recently in history. However, just like the planted grain of wheat, the machine uses resources that might have been consumed instead. Thus foregone consumption is required for machine production just as some bread is foregone now so that more bread can be made in the future.

4. There is one story in Scripture where resources were stored for future consumption and the practice is applauded. Joseph stored seven years of consumption goods in Egypt for use during the coming famine (Gen. 41). This case is an unusual one in which God provided special foresight and was working out a special purpose in history by Joseph's actions. In contrast to this story is the case in the wilderness: any storing of manna for future consumption was sinful (Exod. 16). This is again a special case of God working out a specific objective. It would be inaccurate to teach against future consumption solely on the basis of the wilderness example, just as it would be wrong to teach a positive view of hoarding on the basis of Joseph's case. The entire

scope of biblical teaching must be considered before generalizations are helpful.

5. E. K. Hunt, *Property and Prophets: The Evolution of Economic Institutions and Ideologies*, 4th ed. (Cambridge: Harper and Row, 1981),13.

6. Hunt, 9.

Chapter 6: A Radical Economic Model for Today

1. Each year I teach Consumer Finance to a class of undergraduates. In additional to all the housing, insurance, and budgeting material, there is a major project where students develop a lifetime master financial plan. They are forced to look at their future in terms of values and commitments as well as money. A reasonable retirement and estate plan can insure that one is not building for a lavish future. It can also help one be more intentional about their charity plans. In short, plan well and share your plans with those to whom you are accountable.

2. Henry Rempel, "Our Role in the World Food Crisis," *Church, Industry and Business Association*, July 1976, 5.

3. The barriers created between people by disparate consumption and income levels are illustrated well in an article by Jon Bonk, "The Role of Affluence in the Christian Missionary Enterprise from the West," *Missiology: An International Review* 14, no. 4 (Oct. 1986). Although this article is concerned mainly with foreign mission situations, the message is relevant within cultures as well as between cultures.

4. Leon Lukaszewski, "Let's Get Moral About Money," *U.S. Catholic* 40 (Feb. 1975): 13.

Chapter 7: The Model Illustrated

1. Dave Jackson and Neta Jackson, *Glimpses of Glory: Thirty Years of Community* (Elgin, Ill.: Brethren, 1987). This study is one of several that gives helpful insights into the dynamics of communal living. Another, describing the Woodcrest bruderhof community in New York, is by Ulrich Eggers, *Community for Life* (Scottdale, Pa.: Herald Press, 1980). A historical treatment of communal living is Trevor J. Saxby's *Pilgrims of a Common Life* (Scottdale, Pa.: Herald Press, 1987). See also Luther E. Smith, Jr., *Intimacy and Mission: Intentional Community as Crucible for Radical Discipleship* (Scottdale, Pa.: Herald Press, 1994).

2. Jackson and Jackson, 16.

3. Jackson and Jackson, 314.

Chapter 8: Individual Freedom and Private Property

1. Among the major works of Hayek are *The Constitution of Liberty; Law, Legislation and Liberty* (Chicago: University of Chicago Press, 1960) and *Road to Serfdom* (Chicago: University of Chicago Press, 1944). A small but informative summary of Hayek's ideas can be found in the book by Eamonn Butler, *Hayek* (New York: University Books, 1983). The examples listed in the following paragraphs are found in various sources from Hayek, including *Studies in Philosophy, Politics, and Economics* (Chicago: University of Chicago Press, Midway Reprint Series, 1980), 69-70 (bees); and *The Counter-Revolution of Science: Studies on the Abuse of Reason* (London and New York: The Free Press of Glencoe/Collier-Macmillan, 1955), chap. 4 (footpaths).

2. Cited in Martin Hengel, *Property and Riches in the Early Church: Aspects of a Social History of Early Christianity,* trans. John Bowden (Philadelphia: Fortress, 1974), 1.

Chapter 9: The Harmony of Self-Interested Behavior

1. Bernard Mandeville, *Fable of the Bees,* ed. F. B. Kaye (Oxford: Clarendon, 1924), 24-25.

2. Adam Smith, *An Inquiry into the Nature and Causes of the Wealth of Nations,* ed. Edwin Cannan, 2 vols. (Chicago: University of Chicago Press, 1976), 1:477-478.

3. It is a bit unusual to relate Rawls's theory of justice to Smith's view of sympathy because Rawls's ideas are not focused toward the harmony of self-interested behavior. His principles protecting liberty for all and the welfare of the least advantaged of a group are concerned with societal justice that would complement and go beyond the scope of this book. For a concise treatment of Rawls's work, read "John Rawls" by Alan Ryan in *The Return of Grand Theory in the Human Sciences,* ed. Quentin Skinner (New York: Cambridge University Press, 1985).

4. Paul Heyne, *The Economic Way of Thinking,* 5th ed. (Chicago: Science Research Associates, 1987), 354.

Chapter 10: Limited Government Activity

1. A good place to get a perspective on these issues is from *Earthkeepers: Environmental Perspectives on Hunger, Poverty and Injustice,* by Art and Jocele Meyer (Scottdale, Pa.: Herald Press, 1991); or *Tending the Garden: Essays on the Gospel and the Earth,* ed. Wesley Granberg-Michaelson (Grand Rapids: Eerdmans, 1987); or from the anthology *The Environmental Crisis: The Ethical Dilemma,* ed. Edwin R. Squires (Mancelona, Mich.: AuSable Trails, 1982). The 1982 book contains articles by twenty-six Christian aca-

demic and policy persons on a variety of issues relating to ongoing environmental concerns.

2. Charles Murray, *Losing Ground: American Social Policy 1950-1980* (New York: Basic Books, 1984), 227.

3. Murray, 228.

4. Greg J. Duncan et al., *Years of Poverty, Years of Plenty: The Changing Economic Fortunes of American Workers and Families* (Ann Arbor: Institute for Social Research, 1984).

5. Richard D. Coe and Greg J. Duncan, "Welfare: Promoting Poverty or Progress?" *The Wall Street Journal*, May 15, 1985.

Chapter 12: From Models to Reality

1. Jon Elster, "Social Norms and Economic Theory," *The Journal of Economic Perspectives*, Fall 1989, 99-117.

2. Robert Frank, *Microeconomics and Behavior*, 2nd ed. (New York: McGraw-Hill, 1994), ch. 7.

3. Elizabeth Anderson, "Ethical Limitations of the Market," *Economics and Philosophy*, Oct. 1990, 192.

Chapter 13: Being In the World But Not of It

1. Ronald J. Sider, *Rich Christians in an Age of Hunger* (Waco, Tex.: Word Books, 1990), chap. 3.

2. *The Rich and the Poor: A Christian Perspective on Global Economics,* by Carl Kreider, is one source that will be helpful in developing a global view (Scottdale, Pa.: Herald Press, 1987).

3. Charles P. Kindelberger, *Economic Development*, 3d ed. (New York: McGraw-Hill, 1977), 25.

4. Daniel Bell, *The Cultural Contradictions of Capitalism* (New York: Basic Books, 1976), 176.

Chapter 14: What of the Future?

1. Dennis Farney, "Chaos Theory Seeps into Ecological Debate Stirring Up a Tempest," *Wall Street Journal*, July 8, 1994, 1.

2. David Lyons, *Postmodernity* (Minneapolis: University of Minnesota Press, 1994, 5.

3. Thomas Finger, "Modernity, Postmodernity–What in the World Are They?" *Transformation*, Oct.-Dec. 1993, 24.

4. William F. Allman, "Aternative Realities," *US News & World Report*, May 9, 1994, 60.

5. J. L. Burkholder, "Thinking in a Post Modern Age," (*Goshen College Record*, May 14, 1993, 2.

6. Peter F. Drucker, "The Age of Social Transformation," *Atlantic Monthly*, Nov. 1994, 75.

7. One timely example of this dilemma in the social area is the elimination of planned prayer in public schools. Pluralism demands that no religion be declared as the true one, so we must eliminate officially sponsored prayer completely. In earlier decades, pluralism was bound by such a strong majority of Christian influence that public prayer at school was common. Today we are more diverse, and pluralism demands that no prayer be said publicly lest it elevate one religion to the level of universal truth. Ironically, most Christians see the point and do not demand a Christian prayer. Pluralism and Christian prayers cannot coexist in the same classroom.

8. Farney, 1.

9. Many have already been working to go beyond a narrow rational choice approach to economic behavior. Examples include Robert Frank, Jon Elster, Elizabeth Anderson, Richard Thaler, and Douglas North. The further we can move beyond modeling behavior in purely rationalistic terms, the closer we will get to relating to meaning in economic relationships.

10. The twenty-eight club owners are now insisting that the industry can not survive as it is presently constructed. So what is wrong? The owners claim that baseball does not fit the market scenario. The product is inferior if teams are entering and exiting frequently and revenue depends on emotional ties to teams that will disappear if teams come and go frequently. Also, the physical and social infrastructure of baseball is costly, and so entry and exit is not easy. Nevertheless, small markets with tradition are an important part of the mystique of baseball. Accordingly, the owners' group needs special exceptions to market pressures for the good of the game. They need to manage a revenue-sharing plan that will shift funds from the high-revenue clubs with huge television revenue to the low-revenue clubs in small market areas. Next, because clubs seem to bid too high against each other for players, there must be a cap on how much each team can spend for players. The owners think that this, plus some minor restrictions against unlimited player movements among teams, should make the national pastime the sport it has been over the years. They have convinced most people that the free-market alternative would be chaos, and everyone would lose.

11. Farney, 1.

12. Franey, 1.

13. Franey, 1.

Glossary

AFDC: aid to families with dependent children; part of the federal government's program for helping low-income families.

Anabaptist: often called the third wing of the Reformation. The term was applied in the 1520s to groups that practiced believers baptism on those who already were baptized as infants. The label also was applied to many sects that taught strong separation of church and state and the responsibility of all believers to discern biblical direction in community. Today Mennonites, Brethren, and various other evangelical groups claim this heritage as foundational to their world view.

Antitrust legislation: laws designed to prevent a firm or firms from dominating a market in ways that make the consumer worse off than he would be if many sellers existed in the market. These laws usually restrict the market share of any firm or group of firms in a product area.

Authoritarian social order: A society where a powerful central government dictates how life is ordered. The economic, legal, political, social, and religious functions are planned by the state. Cuba would be a present-day example.

Bureaucratic god: an all-knowing, all-wise, benevolent administrator or central planner who can design an economy to provide the best possible outcomes for the system. Useful as a theoretical construct.

Christian utilitarian modeling: A method of modeling the behavior of Christians which assumes that they still pursue self-interest but that their interest now reflects biblical values. In this view, the utility function changes when one comes to faith. Therefore behavior changes.

Central planning: the practice of having an administrative person or group decide what to produce, how to produce, and to whom the output goes. Market forces and the freedom of the participants in the economy are secondary to the dictates of the planners.

Coercive regulation: government directives to participants m the economy that require specific behavior rather than provide incentive to engage in desired behavior. A law against importing cocaine is an example of this concept; a thousand-dollar-per-ounce tax would be an example of noncoercive regulation.

Competition: a technical term referring to a particular market structure in which many buyers and sellers exist in a given market. No one producer or consumer has power to manipulate price. For example, a producer who tries to raise price above the market rate will sell little if other producers do not increase price also. If other producers were not present the price increase might be wise, but in that case, competition would not be present.

Consumption: using resources that are then not available for any future use. Eating food, attending a concert, burning gasoline for pleasure, and buying jewelry to wear are examples of consumption. Generally those things that make up our standard of living are referred to as consumption goods and services.

Cost-benefit analysis: the process of lining up all costs and all benefits that relate to a decision at hand. Actions with the biggest excess of benefits over costs are selected first in a process, often unconscious, that determines what behavior one undertakes at all points in life. If costs exceed benefits, one rejects that choice. Any assignment of costs and bene-fits is conditioned by one's background, world view, val-ues, peer group, and heritage; behavior is never autono-mously determined.

Countervailing power: the inevitable presence of alternative forces that hold in check groups with power in a society. Labor unions arise to counter management's abuses of power. Producer special-interest groups spring up to check government abuse of power, and consumer special-interest groups form to check both producer and government abuse of power.

Deconstructionism: When one comes to a piece of writing, not with a goal to understand what the author meant, but seeking to interact with it until it becomes meaningful for you, given your situation and values. For a deconstruction-ist, communication is too complex and circumstantial to assume one can glean objective truth from a text.

Democratic capitalism: a market allocative system that is cou-pled with a democratic political system to form a social system characterized by political freedom, limited govern-ment, and free enterprise. The philosophical orientation of this social order comes primarily from the Enlightenment thinking of the eighteenth century.

Deontological: relating to the branch of ethics that emphasizes moral duty, right action, and rules of conduct rather than a utilitarian relativisitic approach to ethics.

Efficiency: the ratio of the value of an output to the value of the inputs used to generate the output. Any value above zero is efficient unless another way of achieving the same result has a higher efficiency rating. A steam engine may be effi-cient, but diesel engines are commonly used because they are more efficient at doing the same task. Since the ratio has value-laden measures in both the numerator and the denominator, it is impossible to use efficiency as an abso-lute measure of what should be done.

FED: the Federal Reserve Board in Washington, D.C., which oversees the Federal Reserve Banking System and engages in monetary policy in order to stabilize the economy.

Fiscal policy: the attempts by the legislative and the executive branches of government to maintain full employment and price stability by making adjustments to the federal budget. Changes in taxation policy or government spending patterns influence various sectors of the economy in ways that push the economy forward away from recession or pull it back from inflationary expansion.

Foundationalism: the view that reality, and therefore science, is built on observable data and that truth can be discerned if the proper methods are used to discover it.

Fractional reserve banking: the practice of banking that requires banks to keep on hand as reserves only a percentage of the money that depositors have put in the bank. This gives flexibility to the money supply, as the FED buys and sells bonds in financial markets to influence the reserves that remain in the accounts of commercial banks.

Free market: the environment in which market participants make independent choices about economic matters. The inputs provided and the output demanded result from choice. There must be enough participants in the market to insure that no one has power over anyone else in determining the level of price or the amount to be exchanged. The term is sometimes used as a synonym for democratic capitalism, but it is best used to describe the more narrow economic subset of that larger social system.

Free riders: those who benefit from economic activity without paying for the benefits they receive. This occurs if two people can consume the same thing without depleting its supply. Community mosquito control is an example where free riding would occur if the market alone is used to provide goods and services. Those who hate mosquitoes most would pay for the control service; everyone enjoys the benefits. Unless the free riders are taxed to help pay for the service, there may be an inadequate level of mosquito control in a community. Each person would wait for someone else to hire the service.

Futures contract an agreement to sell something in the future at a price agreed upon today. The seller of the futures contract has the security of a fixed price, and the buyer has the prospect of a gain should the price of the item rise above the agreed-upon price by the time the exchange occurs.

Hoarding: the practice of putting income into a use that contributes toward neither appropriate consumption for anyone nor an increase in the socially desirable productive capacity of the economy. This is a less-likely occurrence today than in the ancient world, but it can take place when a survivalist mentality leads to stockpiling of goods.

Human capital: education or job training that adds value to basic labor. It is analogous to adding a tool to a productive process. The same financial and ethical investment considerations apply to evaluating a possible investment in human capital or physical capital expenditures.

Hyperspace: a conceptual construct that refers to dimensions of reality that go beyond our four dimensions of length, width, height, and time.

Income redistribution: the shifting of income from one person or group of people to another in ways that change the distribution pattern that would exist if the market distribution alone divided up the pie of production. It has been a goal of capitalist economies to elevate the poor and reduce the economic standing of the rich in ways that appear fair to a majority of the people. Income transfers such as welfare payments and farm subsidies have been used frequently. Property-rights changes involving rezoning or employee stock options is another way to work toward the goal.

Interest: the return on an investment that occurs due to time preference, the productivity of capital, risk absorption, and inflation. The first and third of these sources of interest were most relevant for people in biblical times, although rising prices were not foreign to their understanding. Usury is likely a synonym for interest, although some argue that usury in Scripture refers to extorted returns above the normal rate. This interpretation is not accepted in this book.

Investment: an expenditure on a tool that increases production in a later period. Saving in a bank or buying other financial savings instruments pushes the investment choice on to the person who uses the savings by borrowing the money. During a time when savings cannot all be invested by the economy, they can become a type of hoarding.

Joint consumption: a situation in which more than one person can consume the same good or service with little or no increase in its cost or depletion of its supply. Roads, defense, and parks are a few examples where joint consumption applies. It is customary for these goods to be provided as public goods if it is costly to charge people individually for their use.

Laissez-faire: a term that means a system is self-functioning and needs no outside intervention. A hands-off policy should be followed. The market system is sometimes thought to be this kind of a system, and so the government is not supposed to interfere in market activity.

Loanable funds market: a market for savings that can be loaned to those who need loans. The use of this term in chapter 6 relates to whether huge corporate expenditures for acquisitions reduce the funds available for needed investment in new plants and equipment.

Luxury: an expenditure that elevates one above the living standard that the community of faith has discerned to be appropriate for its witness in the community.

Marginal analysis: the process of approaching a decision by considering only those factors that contribute to the issue at hand. For example, your decision whether or not to sell your used car has nothing to do with the fact that you just spent five hundred dollars to repair the transmission but on whether you think the future costs of keeping the car will outweigh the future benefits of having it. The past is not relevant in effective marginal analysis except as it might help to predict the future. Those who do not use careful thinking on the margin will make poorer decisions than those who do.

Market capitalism: a synonym for democratic capitalism. The dynamics of markets move resources toward the uses they would have if there was one gigantic auction with buyers and sellers offering and accepting bids for good and services. Though very few auctions really occur, resources move in the direction that auctions would dictate if they did exist.

Monetary policy: the tool of the FED to increase or decrease the money supply as desired for stabilization policy.

Multidimensional reality: a way of conceptualizing postmodern reality. The idea that reality is richer than we can know because we are limited to four dimensions. A human being can understand a move downward in dimensions but not an upward move. God's transcendence comes from his existence in dimensions far exceeding human knowledge. Accordingly, we can know only four dimensional truth rather than God's ultimate truth. However, we can claim, in contrast to most postmoderns, that our limited understanding of truth is sufficient for meaning and for movement toward God's higher dimensions after this life.

Neighborhood effects: the impact that production or consumption has on others who are not part of the economic activity under consideration. For example, pollution from a firm impacts the breathing of many who have no relationship to the company or its product. This impact is really part of the cost of the firm's operation, but it is not paid by the company or its customers.

Ownership rights: absolute ownership rights include the deed or title of ownership, the right to use the product of the property, the right to sell the property, and the right to destroy the property. Qualified ownership involves some limitations on one or more of these components. Biblical concepts of ownership emphasize the second of these four rights. The private-property concept of capitalism need not have absolute ownership qualities to function adequately.

Pluralism: the idea that contrasting individual preferences freely expressed are important to a social order and that the resulting diversity will encourage social harmony rather than discord.

Positivism: the philosophical view that knowledge is empirical rather than theological and metaphysical. Theory based on observable facts is the proper way of understanding the world and its social as well as physical systems.

Postmodern: A worldview where reality is subjective and relational. The world is characterized by fragmentation, disorder, and chaos; so people must construct their own reality and find meaning in shared values and relationships. People of similar views become part of a tradition or haven from meaninglessness.

Profit: the difference between the benefits and the costs of a cost-benefit calculation. Is commonly used for the business firm in its financial accounting; the benefits are revenue and the costs are dollar amounts expended for production. In this book the term means net gains from any decision, including those gains from subjective activity.

Public goods: any good or service that is jointly consumed and has a low marginal cost. A large park in the city can be enjoyed by many at once, and the cost of one more person using it is nearly zero. Usually it makes more sense to pay for it with taxes than to fence it off and charge people admission. Thus it is a public good.

Scarcity: a situation in which there is not enough to go around if everything is free. When a price of some kind is paid for a good or service, that is an indication that scarcity exists, because decisions about who gets the goods and services have to be made.

Servanthood motivation of behavior: A method of modeling Christian behavior by assuming believers follow biblical values even though they would prefer to do something else. In this view, behavior changes but the utility function still has some of the old sinful bent in it. One is urged on to servanthood behavior by the expectations of the community of faith and the desire to be a true disciple in spite of the sinful bent of the utility function (2 Cor. 5:14).

Social glue: When all the social institutions of society share values that are complementary rather than contradictory, the social order is viable over time. Those values act as a social glue.

Spreading risk: the act of transferring risk to some person or group that is better prepared to absorb a potential loss. Insurance policies of all kinds and the sale of a futures contract are examples of risk spreading.

Steady-state economy: an economy that maintains a constant population and a constant output level; therefore, the standard of living remains constant as well. The ideal that things will constantly improve is not part of this orientation. Upward social mobility is not acceptable in this type of world since any advance for one will mean a decline for someone else. Much of the ancient and medieval world had this perspective on life.

Subsistence: a standard of living that allows one to stay alive and reasonably well but not to enjoy more than a basic existence. War, disease, and famine were constant threats that thwarted any progress, so subsistence was considered to be the normal state of affairs.

Tariff: a tax on imported goods or services. It has the effect of raising the price of these items, which gives domestic production an advantage in price or the opportunity to increase price also.

Transfer payments: tax receipts that the government gives to persons who need additional income. Welfare payments, farm subsidies, education grants, and social-security payments are examples.

Utility function: A formal statement of the variables from which one derives pleasure.

Worldview: The assumptions one holds about the nature of reality leads to an understanding of how the world works. This understanding is one's worldview, which then guides thought and behavior. For example, the modern worldview is based on Newtonian physics and lead to laissez faire capitalist economics.

Suggested Readings

Beckmann, David. *Where Faith and Economics Meet: A Christian Critique.* Minneapolis: Augsburg, 1981.

Beisner, E. Calvin. *Prosperity and Poverty: The Compassionate Use of Resources in a World of Scarcity.* Westchester, Ill.: Crossway, 1988.

Calvin College Economics Department, *Through the Eye of a Needle: Readings on Stewardship and Justice.* Grand Rapids: Calvin College, 1989.

Chewning, Richard C., ed. *Biblical Principles and Public Policy: The Practice.* Colorado Springs: NavPress, 1991.

Clouse, Robert G., ed. *Wealth and Poverty: Four Christian Views of Economics.* Downers Grove: InterVarsity, 1984.

Davis, John Jefferson. *Your Wealth in God's World: Does the Bible Support the Free Market?* Phillipsburg, N.J.: Presbyterian and Reformed, 1984.

Duncan, Greg J., et al. *Years of Poverty, Years of Plenty: The Changing Economic Fortunes of American Workers and Families.* Ann Arbor: Institute for Social Research, 1984.

Ellul, Jacques. *Money and Power.* Translated by LaVonne Neff. Downers Grove: InterVarsity, 1984.

Elzinga, Kenneth G. "A Christian View of Economic Order." *Reformed Journal* (October 1981): 13-16.

Finn, Daniel R., and Pemberton L. Prentiss. *Toward a Christian Economic Ethic: Stewardship and Social Power.* Minneapolis: Winston, 1985.

Goudzwaard, Bob. *Capitalism and Progress: A Diagnosis of Western Society.* Translated and edited by Josina Van Nuis Zylstra. Grand Rapids: Eerdmans, 1979.

Griffiths, Brian. *The Creation of Wealth: A Christian Case for Capitalism.* Downers Grove: InterVarsity, 1984.

_____ . *Morality and the Marketplace.* London: Hodder and Stoughton, 1982.

Hay, Donald A. *Economics Today: A Christian Critique.* Grand Rapids: William B. Eerdmans, 1989.

Handy, Charles. *The Age of Paradox.* Boston: Harvard Business School Press, 1994.

Hengel, Martin. *Property and Riches in the Early Church: Aspects of a Social History of Early Christianity.* Translated by John Bowden. Philadelphia: Fortress, 1974.

Klay, Robin Kendrick. *Counting the Cost: The Economics of Christian Stewardship.* Grand Rapids: Eerdmans, 1986.

Kreider, Carl. *The Christian Enterpreneur.* Scottdale, Penn.: Herald Press, 1980.

_____. *The Rich and the Poor: A Christian Perspective on Global Economics.* Scottdale, Penn.: Herald Press, 1987.

Lyons, David. *Postmodernity.* Minneapolis: University of Minnesota Press, 1994.

Neuhaus, Richard John. *Doing Well and Doing Good: The Challenge to the Christian Capitalist.* New York: Doubleday, 1992.

Novak, Michael. *The Spirit of Democratic Capitalism.* New York: Simon and Schuster, 1982.

Owensby, Walter L. *Economics for Prophets: A Primer on Concepts, Realities, and Values in Our Economic System.* Grand Rapids: Eerdmans, 1988.

Preston, Ronald H. *Religion and the Ambiguities of Capitalism.* London: SCM Press, 1991.

Redekop, Calvin, ed., et al. *Anabaptist/Mennonite Faith and Economics.* Lanham, Md.: University Press of America, 1994.

Reumann, John, *Stewardship and the Economy of God.* Grand Rapids: William B. Eerdmans, 1992.

Richardson, J. David. "Frontiers in Economics and Christian Scholarship." *Christian Scholar's Review* 17 (June 1988): 4.

Schumacher, E. F. *Small Is Beautiful: Economics As If People Mattered.* New York: Harper and Row, 1973.

Sider, Ronald J. *Rich Christians in an Age of Hunger: A Biblical Study.* 2d rev. ed. Downers Grove: InterVarsity, 1984.

Sine, Tom. *The Mustard Seed Conspiracy.* Waco: Word, 1981.

Storkey, Alan. *Transforming Economics: A Christian Way to Employment.* London: Third Way Books, 1986.

Tamari, Meir. *With All Your Possessions: Jewish Ethics and Economic Activity.* New York: Free Press, 1987.

Vickers, Douglas. *A Christian Approach to Economics and the Cultural Condition.* Smithtown, N.Y.: Exposition, 1982.

Wogaman, J. Philip. *Economics and Ethics: A Christian Inquiry.* Philadelphia: Fortress, 1986.

Wright, Christopher J. H. *An Eye for an Eye: The Place of Old Testament Ethics Today.* Downers Grove: InterVarsity, 1983.

Subject Index

Scripture Index

Author

James Halteman, an economist and educator, is professor of business and economics at Wheaton (Ill.) College. Earlier he taught at Taylor University, Upland, Indiana. His areas of professional study focus on the modeling of economic behavior and the history of economic thought.

Halteman earned a B.A. in history from Goshen (Ind.) College and holds M.A. and Ph.D. degrees in economics from the Pennsylvania State University. He has lectured widely and written the first edition of this book (*Market Capitalism and Christianity*), a *Study Guide to Economics and Behavior*, and numerous articles on economics. Halteman is a member of the American Economic Association, the Association of Christian Economists, Mennonite Economic Development Associates, and the Association of Social Economists.

For twenty years Halteman has been active in Christian education, jointly involved in both the mainstream evangelical world and the Anabaptist world. He has observed contrasts between the two theological orientations and their strengths and weaknesses. His voice clarifies the increasing relevance of the Anabaptist message and the value of ecumenical dialogue.

Halteman is a member of the Lombard (Ill.) Mennonite Church, the Goshen College board of overseers, and the finance commission of the Illinois Mennonite Conference. James was born in Sellersville, Pennsylvania. He and his wife, Jane Bishop, have a son and a daughter, Matthew and Megan.